The Magic of
HERBS

The Magic of
HERBS

JANE NEWDICK

TED SMART

A SALAMANDER BOOK

Specially produced for Ted Smart
Guardian House, Borough Road,
Godalming, Surrey GU7 2AE

ISBN: 1 85613 095 9

CREDITS

EDITOR: Lisa Dyer
DESIGNER: Bridgewater Design Ltd
PHOTOGRAPHER: Di Lewis
TYPESET: Central Southern Typesetters, Eastbourne
COLOUR REPRODUCTION: Scantrans Pte Ltd, Singapore

PRINTED IN HONG KONG

Contents

— • —

Introduction

From the earliest days of civilization, people have grown herbs for basic sustenance and medicinal cures, as well as for the aesthetic and sensory pleasure the growing plants provide. In a strict botanical sense, a herb has no woody tissue and dies down to the ground after the growing season. But today many plants are referred to as herbs when they are used to provide scent, flavour, essential oils and medicinal benefits. The sweet, spicy bay leaf, for example, has been a culinary ingredient and medicinal plant for thousands of years, and the exquisitely scented rose has been revered all over the world for its many fragrant and decorative uses, but neither plant would fit neatly into the true herb category.

In the Middle Ages, herbal plants were cultivated at monasteries, primarily for their medicinal uses, and they then became an integral part of folk medicine until the late seventeenth century. Thanks to the diligence of the monks, and the careful experimentation and discovery of herbs since then, we now have a wonderfully varied choice of herbs to use in many ways.

As part of the long heritage of knowledge passed down from generation to generation, we now use herbs almost without thinking. A sprig of mint tossed into a pot of boiling potatoes, or a handful of parsley in a stuffing for a roast chicken – we consider herbs essential to cooking.

Though many of the original medicinal uses of herbs have become more or less obsolete because of sophisticated modern health care, there are still traditional and old-fashioned ways to use herbs. It seems appropriate to use herbs in time-honoured ways, as they are potent with ancient folklore and superstition. Including herbs in posies and pot-pourris, or making tea, perfume and skin treatments, as well as using herbs to add a unique and pungent taste to food, are all ways herbs have been used since ancient days.

In more recent times, herbs have become appreciated for their decorative qualities in all kinds of gardens, not just herb gardens, and in containers, both indoors and outdoors. They add an extra dimension of scent and colour, as well as a sense of history, which adds to their charm. Herbs are often understated in appearance, but they have a subtle beauty which makes them fit in well among more exotic plants in the flower border. Many well-known herbs have varieties with variegated or brightly coloured foliage, and these varieties add more contrast to a garden.

In the following pages, there are ideas showing you how to make the most of herbs you buy or grow. You may never have tried some of the herbs before, but all the best-known and well-loved herbs are included. Projects and recipes have been derived from a variety of sources; in many countries, certain herbs are highly valued for their use in decoration and cuisine. For example, in France southernwood is used as a moth repellent in *garde-robe* mixtures and posies, and tarragon is an extremely popular French culinary ingredient. As well as many traditional projects using herbs, you will find inspiration for decorative projects using fresh and dried herbs, and details on storing and preserving herbs.

Always be sensible about the quantity of herbs you use in recipes, and the frequency with which you consume herbs, particularly if you are pregnant or have any special health problems. Some herbs have irritating thistles or sap, which should be avoided. Apart from this cautionary note, experiment and have fun with herbs, trying some new flavours and scents, and exploring further the fascinating and intriguing subject of herbs.

FILLED WITH COLOURFUL PLANTS, THIS INFORMAL HERB BORDER EDGES BOTH SIDES OF A PATH, ENABLING THE HERBS TO BE ENJOYED BY ALL WHO PASS BY.

Garlic

ALLIUM SATIVUM

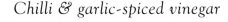

Garlic is a hardy perennial belonging to the onion family. It is an ancient plant which has been used for centuries throughout the world. In medieval times in Great Britain, it was grown extensively for use in the kitchen and as a preventative for the plague. During this period, it was known as gar leek, because the cloves were spear-shaped and 'gar' meant 'spear' in Old English.

Popular taste for the plant seems to have been lost down through the ages, but it has regained favour since tastes in food have become more cosmopolitan and open-minded. It is believed to be a medically beneficial plant, and certainly the regions which use it as an important part of their diet, such as the Mediterranean countries, have some of the healthiest diets today.

Garlic grows as a bulb under the earth. It is easy to cultivate, but it does require a long growing season, plenty of sun, and light, moist soil.

Plant individual cloves in late autumn or early spring. You can buy special garlic for planting or simply use cloves that you have bought for cooking or that are left over from last year's crop.

Harvest the garlic in summer when the grasslike tops have turned brown and dried off. Lift the bulbs, allow them to dry in the sun, and store in a cool, airy outbuilding. When each bulb is ripe, it splits into 10 or more individual cloves covered in a papery skin. Ripe garlic can be stored for up to a year, and then it begins to sprout and lose flavour.

A successful combination is garlic with olive oil. Garlic's astringent qualities do much to cut the fattiness of oils, dairy products and meats. Salads are another area of food where garlic is indispensible, either used in a dressing by combining garlic with other ingredients, or used discreetly by rubbing the salad bowl with garlic.

Chilli & garlic-spiced vinegar

8 whole garlic cloves, peeled
10 small red chillies, fresh or dried
2 tablespoons mustard seed
1 teaspoon allspice berries
1 teaspoon red peppercorns
1 teaspoon coriander seeds
4 small bay leaves
1 pint (600 ml) white wine or cider vinegar

Halve the garlic cloves if they are very large. Put all the ingredients, except the vinegar, into a clean bottle or jar. Pour the vinegar into the bottle through a funnel, and cork or stopper the bottle very firmly. Leave for several weeks. Use for marinades or salad dressings.

SPICY CHILLI AND GARLIC VINEGAR MAKES A USEFUL STORECUPBOARD INGREDIENT, AND IS EXCELLENT IN SALADS, SAUCES, MARINADES AND CASSEROLES.

FRESH GARLIC HAS THE BEST FLAVOUR AND IT CAN BE STORED UNTIL THE FOLLOWING SEASON IF KEPT IN A COOL, AIRY PLACE.

Pot-roasted chicken with garlic

•

SERVES 6

A 4 lb (1.8 kg) fresh, free-range chicken
20 garlic cloves, unpeeled
A sprig each of thyme, parsley and bay leaf
Salt and pepper
A glass of white wine

Put the chicken into a deep casserole dish. Tuck the garlic cloves round and under the chicken. Add the herbs, a little salt and pepper, then pour the glass of wine over the chicken. Cover with a close-fitting lid and put in a hot oven at 200°C (400°F) Mark 6 for 30 minutes. Lower heat to 180°C (350°F) Mark 4 and cook for a further 1½ hours. Lift the chicken from the casserole and keep warm. Skim off fat from the remaining juice and remove herbs. Concentrate the juice by fast boiling to reduce. Serve the chicken surrounded by garlic and hand round juice separately. The garlic cloves will be soft and mellow, and the inside of the clove can be removed and eaten with slices of the chicken.

GARLIC SOFTENS AND MELLOWS WITH COOKING, AND CAN BE EATEN WHOLE, AS IN THIS CHICKEN RECIPE.

Garlic seems to provoke great differences in opinion, and while many people love the taste with a passion, others never let it pass their lips, positive they hate the flavour. But many garlic haters have often eaten dishes which contain garlic without knowing, and have been delighted by how good the flavour is. Raw garlic should be used with some care, as it is very strong; it should be finely chopped or pressed.

Most skilful cooks can crush a clove of garlic with one swipe of a large-bladed knife, but this can be difficult for the amateur. A safer method is to crush the peeled clove with a little salt on a work surface, using the prongs of a fork. Or use a garlic press, which is specially designed for the job, even though it may be troublesome to clean afterward. Make sure you buy garlic that is firm and solid. Store garlic in a dry and airy place.

There are some recipes which are completely reliant upon the special qualities garlic adds. The pungent Provençal aïoli is made from garlic and mayonnaise, and can be eaten with crudités, cooked white fish, or with Mediterranean fish soup. Many Italian-style dishes, such as buttery garlic bread and pasta sauces, are largely based on garlic; some sauces are as simple as crushed garlic, herbs and olive oil.

In other recipes, the whole garlic is used or introduced to flavour the cooking oil. The chicken recipe, above, uses whole garlic cloves. It is a classic French recipe worth reviving and very easy to make. Many stir-fried Chinese recipes instruct to heat ginger and garlic with the oil for the first step of cooking. The ginger and garlic is then discarded once they have added flavour to the oil, and before they turn brown.

Garlic bread

———— • ————

1 long French loaf or 2 round Italian breads
Garlic butter (see right)

Cut bread diagonally without cutting the whole
way through. Spread the garlic butter generously
on each side of the cuts. Wrap in aluminium foil
and heat in a hot oven until the bread is warmed
through, about 10 minutes.

    Alternatively, mix the garlic butter into
freshly made bread dough, and bake the bread
according to the bread recipe.

GARLIC BUTTER

2 large garlic cloves, peeled
6 oz (175 g) butter, softened
1 tablespoon chopped fresh herbs, such as parsley,
    chives, chervil
Salt and pepper

Crush the garlic and add to the softened butter
along with the finely chopped herbs and salt and
pepper. Mix thoroughly.

ONE OF THE BEST
USES FOR GARLIC
BUTTER IS IN GARLIC
BREAD, BUT IT CAN
ALSO BE USED TO
DRESS VEGETABLES.

Chive

ALLIUM SCHOENOPRASUM

The chive is a hardy plant belonging to the onion family, which contains several other useful culinary herbs, such as garlic, onions and shallots. The chive has a taste that is mild and oniony. It is chiefly used as a raw garnish and decoration for all kinds of savoury dishes. The bright green leaves are grass-like and hollow, and appear early, in spring. The plants grow into neat, rounded clumps which make very pretty path edgings and additions to decorative herb gardens. The taller-growing varieties are attractive enough to be included in mixed herbaceous borders where the soft mauve of the globe-shaped flowers hold their own among more dramatic blooms.

Chives are reliably perennial and prefer moist, rich soil in sun or partial shade. They will need frequent watering in dry weather. Plants die down in winter, but reappear the following spring. After a few years, it is wise to replace chive plants with new ones before their growth becomes exhausted. New plants are easily raised from seed sown in spring, and then the small plants can be moved to their permanent home later during the summer. If plants are grown for outdoor decoration and not used much in the kitchen, then a shearing over of the leaves once or twice in the summer, after the flowers have died down, will encourage the clump to replenish itself with new leaves. A chive plant kept near the kitchen door for frequent snipping will stay neat and tidy all year.

Chives have probably been cultivated as garden plants since about the sixteenth century, but they have always tended to be used as an adjunct to food rather than providing their own flavour to food. Chives are thought to help stimulate the appetite and promote good digestion. For best results, they should be used raw.

Many cooked vegetable dishes are enhanced by a discreet sprinkling of snipped chives. The simplest way to do this is to use sharp kitchen scissors rather than a knife which too easily bruises the delicate, hollow leaves. Snipped chives are also delicious mixed with other fresh herbs and stirred through mayonnaise or butter, or added with crushed garlic to soft, fresh cream or curd cheeses.

WITH THEIR GLOBULAR, MAUVE FLOWERS AND BRIGHT GREEN LEAVES, CHIVES MAKE A COLOURFUL DISPLAY IN A HERB GARDEN.

Miniature herbed cheeses

•

MAKES 4 CHEESES

*Chives have a natural affinity with mild, fresh
cheeses. Use any fresh, soft curd or cream cheese,
such as cow's, goat's or sheep's milk cheese.*

*A large handful of fresh chives
8 oz (225 g) soft cheese
½ garlic clove, crushed (optional)
Salt and pepper*

Snip all but 8 long chive leaves into tiny pieces.
In a bowl, combine the cheese, snipped chives,
garlic and salt and pepper. Mix until well
blended. With your hands, quickly make 4
round shapes from the cheese. Using the
remaining long chive leaves, tie each cheese
with 2 leaves, like a parcel. Leave for several
hours in a cool place for the flavours to develop.
Serve individually as a savoury dessert, or with a
selection of other cheeses, alongside plain
oatcakes or water biscuits.

THE MILD ONION FLAVOUR OF CHIVES COMPLEMENTS SOFT
CHEESES. HERE, LONG CHIVES HAVE BEEN USED LIKE
DECORATIVE RIBBONS ROUND EACH CHEESE.

Dried chives are widely available but are generally not worth buying, as the taste and texture
are very far removed from the fresh version.
Chives are not very successful frozen either, so it
is really best to enjoy them fresh. With a little
care, they are available for a long season in the
garden, and they are now easy to buy all year
round as cut herbs. Chives are a very satisfactory
herb to grow in a pot or window-box for those
who do not have a garden, provided they are
frequently watered and the leaves are regularly
harvested to promote a steady growth.

Chives must rank among the three or four
most useful culinary herbs to have for garnishing
many different dishes. The colour contrast of
bright green chives always looks attractive combined with deep purple beetroot or with raw
salads based on brilliant orange, grated carrot.
Good, ripe, red tomatoes, sliced and dressed
with oil, always benefit from the subtle onion
flavour of scattered chives.

The pretty chive flowers are edible as well as
the leaves, and they appear in the middle of
summer. Chive flowers can be added whole or
pulled apart to salads of mixed lettuce leaves.
They add a decorative touch when floated on
cold, creamy soups or on a chive-flavoured sauce.
Whole chive flowers, with their rose or purple
colours, also make a vibrant garnish on a serving
dish or individual plate.

SCATTER CHIVES
AND COARSE SALT
OVER BUTTERED
NEW POTATOES
COOKED IN THEIR
SKINS TO ADD A
SPECIAL TOUCH TO A
SIMPLE DISH.

Chives are used successfully with potatoes. Baked potatoes served with sour cream and chives is a traditional side dish, and new potatoes, steamed in their skins and glistening with butter, are beautifully decorated with a handful of chives. Cold potato salad, made from delicious waxy potatoes in a home-made French dressing or light mayonnaise and scattered with chives, is another favourite for picnics or other meals.

Chives make a classic partnership with eggs cooked in a variety of ways. Cocottes of baked eggs, cream and chives are simply delicious. Or mix chopped boiled egg and chives for sandwich fillings for lunch-time meals. Scatter chives over lightly scrambled eggs, or use them in a mixture for soufflés. Chives can also be used to make an excellent herb butter; melt the butter over fish or any vegetable dish. To make the butter, simply pound a handful of chives with unsalted butter in a mortar (or use a liquidizer or food processor) and shape the butter into small, round pats. Herb butter will keep frozen if tightly sealed.

Chives add a gentle flavour, with just enough bite, to mild vegetable cream soups, particularly ones based on peas or potatoes. They are the classic garnish for vichyssoise, served either hot or cold, which is a soup made from leeks and potatoes (see recipe right). Several long lengths of chive leaf look pretty curled elegantly on the surface of a soup or sauce. It is easiest to do this by splitting and separating the chives into two halves, which will then curve more easily.

Classic leek & potato soup

•

SERVES 4 — 6

Traditionally this creamy and soothing soup is served chilled, but it is also perfect for eating hot on cold winter days.

2 lb (900 g) leeks
1 lb (450 g) potatoes
2 oz (50 g) butter
1 pint (600 ml) chicken or vegetable stock
1 pint (600 ml) milk
Salt and pepper
Grated nutmeg
Single cream (optional)
Snipped chives, to decorate

Clean and slice leeks, and peel and chop potatoes. Melt the butter in a large saucepan and add the vegetables. Cook gently over a low heat for about 5 minutes, stirring constantly. Add stock and milk, and bring to the boil. Season with salt, pepper, and a little nutmeg.

Simmer uncovered for about 20 minutes, until the vegetables are just tender. Sieve or liquidize the mixture for a smooth soup, or process in a food processor for a slightly more textured version. Either reheat if serving warm, or put in a cool place to chill for several hours if serving cold. When serving, swirl in a little single cream, if you desire, and scatter each serving with a generous garnish of chopped chives and several chive flowers if you have them.

PALE CREAMY SOUPS, SUCH AS THIS LEEK AND POTATO SOUP, BENEFIT FROM A SPRINKLING OF SNIPPED CHIVES TO ADD FLAVOUR AND COLOUR.

Dill

ANETHUM GRAVEOLENS

This delicate herb from the umbellifer family obtains its name from 'dillian', meaning 'to lull' in the ancient Saxon language. Dill is still used today in preparations for babies, to calm digestive problems and to soothe them to sleep. Another common name for the herb is dilly.

Both the soft, feathery leaves and the ripe seeds of the plant are used to provide a mild aniseed flavour, not unlike fennel. The dried seeds are stronger in taste than the leaves, and they are commonly used for flavouring pickles, particularly ones made from gherkins and cucumber. In Scandinavian cooking, dill is often used with fresh and preserved fish, with which it has a great affinity. It is also frequently used in Russian cooking, especially with the classic beetroot soup, borscht. Nowadays, dill is used more often only as a decorative and edible garnish.

Dill is a fairly easy plant to grow, but it is small and likely to get lost among larger plants, so grow it in a small patch of its own. It is a hardy annual and can be grown from seed in spring and successively throughout the summer. Once it has flowered, it seeds quickly, and then the foliage is no longer very suitable for cutting. Keep dill growing persistently with moisture, good soil, and in a light but sheltered position.

Dill is one of the few herbs which freezes quite well but, unfortunately, the texture is spoiled. It is normally added near the end of cooking a dish or else just used as a raw garnish. Though it has a lovely, mild flavour, do not use it with a heavy hand as its subtlety should be enjoyed. Try it with beetroot dishes where it combines well with the sweetness of these vegetables, and add it to sauces and dressings for all kinds of fish dishes.

GRAVAD LAX RELIES ON PLENTY OF FRESH DILL FOR ITS UNIQUE FLAVOUR. THE ACCOMPANYING SAUCE CAN ALSO BE EATEN WITH SMOKED TROUT OR MACKEREL.

Apple, celery & dill salad

Dill adds a fresh-tasting flavour to an apple and salad to eat with pickled rollmop herrings.

Simply combine equal quantities of cubed, cored, red-skinned eating apples with crisp, chopped celery. Toss the salad with a salad dressing made from olive oil, lemon juice and 1 tablespoon of chopped fresh dill. Serve the salad immediately, as part of a light lunch or snack.

FRESH DILL COMBINES BEAUTIFULLY WITH FISH. HERE, MARINATED ROLL-MOP HERRINGS ARE ACCOMPANIED BY A CRUNCHY APPLE, CELERY AND DILL SALAD.

Gravad lax with mustard & dill sauce

SERVES 6—8 AS A STARTER

It is possible to buy the salmon already pickled, but home-cured salmon is far more delicious. Make the dressing and store any extra in a glass jar in the refrigerator for another meal.

A 3—4 lb (1.4—1.8 kg) piece of fresh salmon
2 tablespoons sea salt
2 tablespoons sugar
2 teaspoons crushed black peppercorns
2 tablespoons brandy
2 tablespoons chopped fresh dill

Cut the salmon piece into half lengthwise. Remove all the bones but leave the skin intact. Mix all the other ingredients together and put one quarter of the mixture on a large, shallow plate. Put 1 salmon fillet, skin-side down, on the dish and spread with half of the remaining pickle mixture. Lay the second salmon fillet on top of the first, skin-side up. Rub the remaining pickle mixture on to the skin. Cover the fish with aluminium foil and place a flat board across the top. Place a weight, weighing at least 4 lb (1.8 kg), on the board. Leave in the refrigerator for up to 5 days to cure. Serve thinly sliced with the mustard and dill sauce.

MUSTARD & DILL SAUCE

1 egg yolk
2 tablespoons prepared French mustard
1 tablespoon sugar
2 tablespoons white wine vinegar
6 tablespoons olive oil
1 tablespoon finely chopped, fresh dill
Salt and pepper

Beat egg yolk, mustard and sugar together until smooth. Add vinegar, then oil, bit by bit, beating well until a good consistency is attained. Fold in the dill and season with salt and pepper.

Angelica

ANGELICA ARCHANGELICA

·

Angelica is slightly unusual among herbs because it is one of the few which is now only used for sweet dishes. The herb takes its name from the Archangel Michael, partly because it was thought to always bloom on 8 May, a day when he is said to have appeared in a monk's vision during the Middle Ages and announced that the herb would cure the black plague. Old references to the herb suggest that it was taken for stomach disorders and that all the parts, including the roots, of the plant were used.

Angelica is most often used as a candied decoration and a flavouring for puddings and cakes. The flavour of the plant is somewhat similar to that of juniper berries and the leaves are noticeably aromatic. Fresh stems picked in spring can be made into sugar-coated, candied angelica. The root and leaves can be cooked fresh, with rhubarb or apple to reduce the acidity.

HERE ARE GLACÉ FRUITS AND CANDIED ANGELICA. SMALL PIECES OF THE ANGELICA CAN BE USED TO GARNISH DESSERTS OR INCLUDED IN RECIPES FOR SWEET DISHES.

As a garden plant, angelica is statuesque and very architectural. It produces enormous, yellowish, typically umbellifer, flowers in the second summer. It then dies down, but usually self-seeds near the original plant. Plant angelica at the back of a herb garden or border, or use it as a focus plant beside a building, at the end of a vista, or in the centre of a formal herb garden.

Candied angelica

·

Stems for candying should be young and tender. You can easily multiply or divide the ingredients below to suit the amount of angelica you have.

1 lb (450 g) angelica stems
1 lb (450 g) plus 4 oz (100 g) sugar
Water

Cut the angelica stems into pieces, each about 4 inches (10 cm) long, and simmer in water for about 20 minutes, until tender. Remove from the water and strip off the outer skin on each piece. Then return the pieces to the pan for a second simmering, about 10 minutes. Drain the cooked stems and layer in a china bowl, alternating with equal amounts of the 1 lb (450 g) of sugar. Leave for 2 days.

At the end of 2 days, put the stems and sugar back into a saucepan filled with water and simmer for 30 minutes or so. Remove angelica and add the remaining 4 oz (100 g) of sugar to the pan. Boil the angelica in this stronger syrup for about 7 minutes more. Drain the stems. Put in a warm place, or a very cool oven with the door ajar, to dry. Store the angelica between sheets of greaseproof paper in a dry place.

Pear & angelica tarts

MAKES 6

This is a wonderful pudding to eat on cool autumn days. Serve the tarts fresh, when just cool.

9 oz (250 g) ready-made sweet shortcrust pastry
3 dessert pears
Sugar
Water
Custard (see right)
Angelica, candied and chopped

Line 6 individual tart tins with the pastry and part-bake blind for 10 minutes. Peel pears and core, but leave the stems attached. Cut each pear in half. Poach pears in a light sugar and water mixture until just tender. Drain the pears and reduce the syrup by fast boiling to make a glaze. Place a pear half in each tart shell, pour over a little custard, and sprinkle some chopped, candied angelica on each one. Bake in a 200°C (400°F) Mark 6 oven for about 15 minutes. Let tarts cool slightly, then brush with pear-syrup glaze. Serve when just cool.

CUSTARD

½ pint (300 ml) milk
2 egg yolks
2 tablespoons plain flour

To make the custard, mix the egg yolks with the flour. Then warm the milk in a saucepan and pour it over the egg yolk mixture, beating constantly. Return mixture to the pan and cook over a low heat until just thickened. Use immediately.

19

Chamomile

ANTHEMIS NOBILIS

The name chamomile is sometimes confusing, covering several different plants, all with similar qualities, including the mayweeds (*Anthemis cotula*), feverfews (*Chrysanthemum parthenium*), and other varieties and hybrids in the *Anthemis* genus. They all have scented foliage and pretty white daisy flowers with yellow eyes. *Anthemis nobilis* is sometimes called Roman chamomile, and the plant has certainly been in use for centuries. The leaves are finely dissected and the stem is procumbent. It is found in dry fields and round cultivated areas. Today chamomile is probably the most widely used plant for herbal tea, but it is also used in liqueurs and wines.

The non-flowering variety of chamomile, called 'Treneague', is low-growing and used to make a scented alternative to grass lawns. It will withstand a certain amount of crushing and can be walked upon. In medieval times, banks and seats were planted with thyme and chamomile to make fragrant garden benches. The benches were designed to be sat upon and crushed, so the scent would be released. The flowering chamomiles, both single and double types, make a pretty addition to a mixed flower border or herb garden, and the bright, cheerful flowers are in bloom for a long period during the year. To successfully grow chamomile, plant it on light, sandy soil in a sunny position. The non-flowering types can only be propagated from cuttings, while the others can be grown from seed.

The German, or wild, chamomile, *Matricaria chamomilla*, is native to southern Europe, but is also cultivated. It has scented flowers, however, the leaves are scentless. This plant is an annual and is grown mainly for its flower production to use as a tisane. Infusions are generally made using the dried flower heads which store well, so are always at hand. It is similar to Roman chamomile in appearance, and its round, hollow stem may be either procumbent or upright.

The word chamomile is derived from a Greek word meaning 'apple', and the leaves do smell similar to green apples. The antiseptic qualities of the leaves were once put to use as insect repellents and clothes fresheners. The blue oil, which was obtained from the plant, was added to baths to soothe and refreshen and it was used in a lotion to bathe inflamed and sore skin. The oil is still said today to be a helpful topical pain reliever, benefiting sensitive, dry and delicate skin. A hair rinse made from chamomile has the properties of lightening and brightening blonde hair over a period of use. Chamomile is often an ingredient in commercial herbal shampoos. To enjoy the relaxing effect of chamomile, use the herb in little bags for the bath.

THE WHITE DAISY FLOWERS OF CHAMOMILE MAKE A BEAUTIFUL AND NATURAL-LOOKING DISPLAY IN A GREEN JAR.

CHAMOMILE TEA IS THE PERFECT NIGHT-TIME DRINK, AS IT ENCOURAGES RELAXATION AND PEACEFUL SLEEP.

Chamomile tea

Chamomile tea is claimed to relax and to sooth digestion, but it should never be drunk to excess. To make the tea, infuse a spoonful of dried chamomile flowers in a teapot of boiling water. After a few minutes, strain the liquid into a cup, to which can be added a slice of lemon, if desired, or a spoonful of clear honey to sweeten the drink. Drink the tea after a meal as a digestive or at night to relax and encourage sleep. For a gift idea, you may like to put dried chamomile flowers in a pretty box or tin and label it, explaining how to make the tea.

Chamomile bath bags

1 tablespoon dried chamomile leaves or flowers
1 tablespoon dried thyme
½ tablespoon dried rosemary
1 tablespoon dried rose petals
6 tablespoons oatmeal

Crumble the dried herbs and mix them in a bowl with the oatmeal. Spoon the mixture into little muslin or cheesecloth bags and tie or sew the open end closed. Hang from the tap in the bath, or simply swirl a few times through the hot water before bathing.

Chervil

ANTHRISCUS CEREFOLIUM

Chervil is a dainty, fern-leaved biennial, grown more often as an annual to provide fresh leaves throughout the year. It resembles flat-leaved parsley and is often used for similar purposes in the kitchen. The flavour of chervil is more delicate than parsley, with a hint of aniseed, which combines beautifully with fish and egg dishes, or in salads, soups, stuffings and vegetable recipes.

The plant grows to about 12 inches (30.5 cm) high and has clusters of white umbellifer flowers. Pinch out the flower buds when they appear, if you want healthy leaves rather than seeds. Though successful in a sunny position, chervil is happier in partial shade through the hottest summer months. For outdoor crops, seeds should be sown in succession throughout the spring and summer where they are to grow. Another option is to grow them in a seed tray and then transplant out of doors. It is also possible to sow seed between autumn and the middle of winter and grow the plants on a light window-sill or in a greenhouse in pots. The leaves will be ready about six to eight weeks after sowing.

Chervil is not one of the most commonly used culinary herbs today, but it is very popular in France where it appears in an important role in the mixture known as *fines herbes*. This is made by mixing equal amounts of chives, tarragon, chervil and parsley together, but it can be adapted by using the fresh herbs you have available and by using the flavours you prefer. The flavour of chervil is lost by long cooking, so always add it at the last moment. It makes a quick and delightful sauce for chicken or fish; just add fresh chervil and a little single cream to the pan juices after cooking and pour the sauce over the dish.

Chervil combines well with eggs; simply scatter chopped chervil over creamy scrambled eggs or bake eggs in cream with chervil. Light, egg-rich pancakes with chervil mixed into the batter are delicious; serve them like blinis with sour cream and, perhaps, a fresh tomato sauce. The classic omelette *fines herbes* (see recipe right) is often overlooked, but it is one of the most wonderful ways to celebrate fresh herbs. The omelette will make a simple lunch or supper.

Omelette fines herbes

•

Use free-range and very fresh eggs as the final result is completely dependent on the quality of ingredients.

2–3 fresh eggs per person
Salt and pepper
Unsalted butter
2 tablespoons of chopped, fresh fines herbes (chervil, tarragon, flat-leaved parsley and chive mixture)

Beat room-temperature eggs lightly and season with salt and pepper. Melt a knob of butter in an omelette or frying pan. Wait until it foams, then begins to subside. Pour in the eggs and cook over a high heat, lifting the edges of the omelette and tipping uncooked egg underneath.

When the omelette is set, but still creamy on the surface, scatter half the *fines herbes* mixture on top. Cook for a few seconds more and fold the omelette over in half. Place on a warm plate and dust with the remaining *fines herbes*. Serve with French bread or warm wholemeal rolls, and follow with a salad.

Chervil soufflés

•

SERVES 4

1½ oz (40 g) butter
1 oz (25 g) flour
½ pint (300 ml) milk
4 eggs, separated
4 tablespoons chopped, fresh chervil
1 tablespoon snipped chives
Salt and pepper
Single cream (optional)

Preheat oven to 190°C (375°F) Mark 5. Melt the butter in a saucepan and add flour, mixing gently. Cook for a few minutes, then gradually add the milk to make a thick sauce. Stir in egg yolks, chervil, chives and salt and pepper. Whisk the egg whites until stiff, then fold into the mixture. Pour into 4 well-greased, individual soufflé dishes and bake for 10–12 minutes until risen and puffy. Serve immediately with some warmed single cream with chervil added, if desired. The soufflés make a perfect starter.

A BEAUTIFULLY SIMPLE AND DELICIOUS OMELETTE MADE FROM FRESH EGGS IS ENHANCED WITH CHERVIL AND OTHER HERBS.

Southernwood

ARTEMISIA ABROTANUM

———— • ————

Southernwood has an interesting aroma like no other plant. It has long been a favourite feature in cottage gardens, and has been known by the common names of old man, lad's love and boy's love. A sprig or two of this herb were, at one time, always included in lover's posies. Its use in pot-pourris and as a moth repellent gives it the name *garde-robe* in France.

Southernwood is a native of southern Europe, and thrives in well-drained soil in a sunny position. It grows to a shrubby bush about 3 feet (90 cm) tall, made up of erect branches covered in ferny, greyish green leaves. It is believed to have been one of the first plants to be introduced into the United States from England, and was mentioned in manuscripts dating back to the ninth century, in which the herb was described as being good for wounds.

One of southernwood's many properties was believed to be the ability to cure baldness, and the name lad's love is probably a reference to the herb being used as a stimulant for the growth of a beard. In medieval times, plants which resembled certain parts of the human body were used to cure illnesses of these body parts, and the leaves of southernwood are often described as hair-like. There is no doubt, though, that the plant does have a special astringent quality. At various times in history it has been used as a cure for sleeplessness and to draw out deep-seated splinters or thorns.

Southernwood, with its soft, grey foliage, makes a lovely plant for any part of the garden. Traditionally, it is planted just inside the garden gate. Early in spring, the previous year's growth should be cut back almost to ground level, then the silvery fronds of new leaf will appear quickly and grow into a rounded and compact bush. Failure to keep the bush in shape results in an ungainly and straggly plant.

There are several other close relatives of southernwood. Wormwood (*Artemisia absinthium*) has deeply dissected, silvery grey leaves. Wormwood was once used in the drink absinthe. Beach wormwood (*Artemisia stelleriana*) is commonly named old woman or dusty miller, and this plant has almost white leaves. It is grown as a perennial and thrives in coastal areas.

Southernwood is a wonderful herb to dry for sweet bags and dried arrangements. Early summer is the best time to pick bunches of the leaves for this purpose. Hang the picked stems in loose bundles in a dark, warm and airy place until they are crisp and completely dry. If the leaves are to be used in moth bags or pot-pourri mixtures, rub them between your fingers to crumble them. Whole dried stems can be left as they are for using in dried posies and arrangements.

BEACH WORMWOOD IS A RELATIVE OF SOUTHERNWOOD, AND MAKES A MORE ORNAMENTAL GARDEN PLANT WITH ITS DEEPLY LOBED, ALMOST WHITE, LEAVES.

SOUTHERNWOOD IS A TRADITIONAL HERB TO USE IN SACHETS AND SMALL POSIES FOR WARDROBES AND BLANKET CHESTS, AS IT DETERS MOTHS AND INSECTS FROM STORED LINEN.

Southernwood posy

To make a dried posy to hang among clothes or in a cupboard, take several stems of dried lavender and a few stems of dried red roses. Tie them together with a small bunch of dried southernwood and complete with a decorative bow. Do not forget to make a loop with the bow so you can hang the posy. Another idea is to fill small muslin bags with a southernwood pot-pourri and place the bags among stored blankets and linen to repel moths.

Southernwood moth bags

1 cup dried southernwood
1 cup dried rosemary
1 cup dried lavender
¼ cup ground cloves
¼ cup crushed cinnamon bark

Combine all the ingredients thoroughly and put the mixture in small bags or sachets. These make lovely gifts when packed into a pretty box, but do label them and explain their function.

French Tarragon

ARTEMISIA DRACUNCULUS

It is important to be sure that you have the right variety of tarragon if you want to use the leaves for cooking. *Artemisia dracunculus* is known as French tarragon, or more commonly just tarragon, and this is the one with the true flavour. Another variety, *Artemisia dracunculoides* or Russian tarragon is similar in appearance, but has hardly any flavour at all; it is altogether a coarser plant. French tarragon is a hardy perennial which should survive all but the hardest winter weather once it is established. Given time, it will develop into a large plant producing many leaves. The leaves die down during the winter, and it is wise to cover over the base of the plant with straw or mulch to protect the roots from hard frosts.

Tarragon should be planted in a warm sheltered site in light, sharply draining soil. As it does not set seed in temperate climates, it is normally propagated by cuttings or divisions from a large plant. It is an untidy-looking plant, grown for its usefulness in the kitchen rather than its attractiveness in the garden. It is one of the top 10 herbs or so that every cook should grow if possible.

Tarragon dip

½ pint (300 ml) fromage frais or any fresh, soft,
    low-fat cheese
1 tablespoon olive oil
1 tablespoon lemon juice
1 small garlic clove, crushed
A handful of fresh tarragon
Salt and pepper

Blend all the ingredients together in a liquidizer or food processor. The mixture should be smooth and all the ingredients thoroughly combined. Spoon into a small dish and serve with a selection of raw vegetables, such as carrots, mange-tout, radishes and peppers.

IN THIS RECIPE, FRESH TARRAGON FLAVOURS A REFRESHING DIPPING SAUCE. SERVE THE DIP WITH A SELECTION OF COLOURFUL RAW VEGETABLES.

Tarragon leaves are strongly flavoured. They are at their best early in the season when they are still young and fresh. The herb should be used alone in dishes, so the delightful flavour will not compete with other flavours. Use tarragon to make dips and sauces for both hot and cold food.

Tarragon is often sold dried or freeze-dried, but it is less desirable in these forms. Rather than attempting to make a tarragon-flavoured dish using dried leaves, capture the flavour of the fresh herb by making a herb vinegar to use throughout the winter months.

Tarragon vinegar

•

Buy or pick bunches of fresh tarragon. Push the whole stems into clean bottles or jars and fill with white wine or cider vinegar. Cork the bottles tightly and leave in a warm place for 2–3 weeks. When the flavour is strong enough, strain the vinegar, removing the herbs. Then re-bottle and add 1 pretty stem of tarragon to each bottle. Store in a cool, dark place, or label and give as presents. The vinegar can be used in salad dressings and sauces.

Tarragon & tomato soup
·

SERVES 4—6

*This soup is delicious served chilled, but could be gently heated if the day is chilly
and a cold soup seems unsuitable.*

1½ lb (700 g) ripe tomatoes
2 tablespoons olive oil
5 spring onions, roughly chopped
1 pint (600 ml) chicken or vegetable stock
3 tablespoons chopped, fresh tarragon
Salt and pepper

Skin the tomatoes by pouring boiling water over them, then plunging into cold water and peeling off the skin. Roughly chop the tomato flesh. Heat the oil in a large saucepan and add the spring onions. Cook for a few minutes over a medium heat but do not allow the onions to brown. Add the tomatoes and cook briefly. Pour on the stock and add half the tarragon. Bring to the boil, then simmer for 15 minutes.

Purée the soup in a liquidizer or pass through a sieve. Season to taste and add the remaining tarragon. Either leave to chill for several hours or reheat gently and serve. Wholemeal bread croûtons make a good contrast of textures if served with the soup.

Chicken with tarragon

SERVES 6

2 oz (50 g) butter
1 medium onion, finely chopped
A 4 lb (1.8 kg) roasting chicken, cut into pieces
A small bunch of fresh tarragon, finely chopped
A small glass of white wine
¼ pint (150 ml) single cream

Melt the butter in a frying pan, and fry the chopped onion for a few minutes until soft and golden. Remove onions and quickly fry each chicken piece until sealed and slightly brown. Transfer the chicken and onion to a shallow baking dish and add the tarragon.

Bake in a moderate oven at 180°C (350°F) Mark 4 for about 1 hour, basting several times with the juices. About 10 minutes before the end of the cooking time, pour the wine over the chicken and then the cream. Return to the oven and finish cooking. Serve from the dish with a scattering of extra chopped tarragon on top.

This dish will need plain and simple accompaniments, such as a green salad and steamed new potatoes or spinach noodles.

CHICKEN AND TARRAGON ARE WONDERFUL CULINARY PARTNERS. IN THIS RECIPE, TARRAGON IS BAKED WITH THE CHICKEN TO MAKE A DELICIOUS SUMMER DISH.

RIPE TOMATOES AND TARRAGON BLEND TOGETHER PERFECTLY IN A RICHLY FLAVOURED AND TEXTURED SOUP. THE SOUP CAN BE SERVED EITHER HOT OR COLD.

In French cooking, there are several distinctive recipes which rely on the special taste of tarragon. One of the best combinations is chicken and tarragon. There are many versions of this popular dish, from cold, poached chicken pieces with a *chaudfroid* sauce to whole roasted birds basted with butter and tarragon. The recipe above is loosely based on a French dish; the chicken pieces are baked simply and the flavour of tarragon is accentuated.

Recipes for sauces, such as béarnaise and hollandaise, frequently include tarragon as an ingredient. The herb is also often tied in a parcel with other herbs for use as a bouquet garni. This little herb parcel adds flavour to meat dishes and soup stocks and is removed before serving.

Another way to add tarragon to food is in a herb butter. The butter makes a beautiful finishing touch to simply cooked vegetables and plainly grilled fish and meat. Chop tarragon finely and beat it into twice its weight of unsalted butter. The butter can be melted or chilled, but is especially good when melted over solid, textured fish, such as turbot, monkfish, brill or bass. Also try the butter with boiled vegetables.

In addition to fish and chicken, tarragon also marries well with egg and beef dishes, though it can be used successfully with many other types of food. Once classic pairing is tarragon with tomatoes, and the recipe for soup, left, is ideal for the summer season when outdoor tomatoes reach their peak of flavour.

Borage

BORAGO OFFICINALIS

Borage is an ancient herb that has been grown for centuries, particularly for its reputed qualities to invigorate, refresh and bring courage. Common names for the pretty blue-flowered plant include bee-bread, because it is a great attraction to bees, cool tankard, for the cucumber taste it brings to drinks, and herb of gladness, which refers to the supposedly cheering effects that the plant gives when it is eaten. The name borage, from the Latin *borago,* probably originated from *borra* or *burra,* meaning 'rough hairs'. The plant is also sometimes known as bugloss and burage.

Borage is strictly an annual plant, but one which seeds itself with such abandon that, once planted, seedlings will appear all round the original spot. Seed should be sown out of doors in early spring to flower later that summer. Self-sown plants from a previous year often overwinter and flower earlier in the summer. Borage thrives in well-drained soil in a sunny location. It looks particularly attractive grown high on a bank or rock garden. The leaves are coarse and bristly, covered with rough, silvery hairs, and the whole plant branches into a big, ungainly bush. Clusters of the deep blue, pendant, star-shaped flowers with black centres smother the plant. A fresh crop of flowers appears every few days during the flowering season.

Nectarine & borage salad

THIS SIMPLE DISH OF SLICED NECTARINES IS SCATTERED WITH THE BLUE STARS OF BORAGE FLOWERS.

At the height of summer, when fruit is at its best and most plentiful, make a simple fruit salad with borage. Wash nectarines and slice them into thin segments. They look best with the deep red skin left on the orange flesh.

Layer the slices in a deep bowl, adding just a light sprinkling of lime or lemon juice. Scatter the surface with a handful of fresh borage flowers and serve the fruit salad immediately. The colour contrast between the deep orange and red of the nectarines and the brilliant blue of the borage is superb.

For a variation, substitute peaches for the nectarines, but skin them first by dipping the fruit in boiling water for about 1 minute, then peeling off the skins before slicing.

A REFRESHING ICED CIDER CUP, IDEAL FOR OUTDOOR SUMMER PARTIES, REQUIRES FRESH BORAGE FOR CUCUMBER TASTE AND PRETTY DECORATION.

All parts of the plant are perfectly safe to eat, so the little flowers can be added to salads, fruit dishes and drinks as edible decorations. The taste of the leaves is a subtle cucumber flavour, which is cool and refreshing. Young shredded leaves can be used in a mixed leaf salad, but avoid using large pieces, as the leaves can be too rough and coarse to eat in sizeable quantities.

If you have an abundance of borage flowers, freeze them to add to cool drinks and punches. Simply place a flower in each compartment in an ice-cube tray and fill with spring water. This idea will work for all kinds of edible flowers and petals, particularly if they are colourful.

Summer cider cup

•

1 pint (600 ml) dry cider
1 liqueur glass Cointreau
Sliced lemons, oranges and strawberries
3 strips cucumber peel
10 borage leaves, shredded
1 pint (600 ml) fizzy mineral water

Pour the cider and Cointreau into a large bowl. Add fruit, cucumber peel and borage leaves. Chill for 1 hour or so. Fill the rest of the bowl with mineral water and ice cubes to taste. Pour into a large jug and decorate with borage flowers.

Marigold

CALENDULA OFFICINALIS

———•———

Although the marigold is chiefly grown as a decorative garden flower, it does, in fact, have a long history as a kitchen herb. In medieval times, it was one of the most important plants grown in the garden, and both the fresh and dried petals were used in the home.

The single-flowered, deep orange pot marigold is more commonly replaced today by double versions in a range of colours, such as pale cream, burnt orange and golden yellow. Grow some of the newer varieties for the garden or for indoor decorations, but try to get seed of the old-fashioned, original version for cooking.

A few marigold plants growing in a mixed herb garden of mainly green plants make a splash of contrasting orange, which is often very welcome. Marigolds are hardy annuals and simple to grow. The leaves are long and narrow, light green in colour, and the stem is branched and hairy.

Both leaves and stems have a pungent odour. The flowers are bright and round. Marigolds are happy in most soils in a sunny part of the garden. They seed themselves recklessly; once you have grown some, you will find more appearing the next year. Sow seed in early spring and thin out the plants so they can spread. The plants sometimes continue flowering right to the end of the year if the weather is mild.

Marigolds in all shades make lovely, bright, summer flower arrangements. They last well in water and look beautiful, either used alone or mixed with other vibrantly coloured flowers. Their only minor disadvantage is that they have rather short stems, so cannot be used in large-scale arrangements. When choosing a container, ensure that the proportion between the vase and the flowers is sympathetic. The dried flowers also make lovely additions to pot-pourris.

The marigold is a common sight in India. It is used to decorate Hindu temple altars and for making flower garlands to place round statues of the gods. The petals have been used for centuries as an inexpensive substitute for saffron, though they taste quite different from that rare spice. The substance in marigold petals that produces the yellow colour is called calendulin. It is similar to carotin in its colouring properties, but the flavour from the volatile oils is slightly bitter. This spicy, peppery flavour was used, at one time, in cheeses, soups, stews, and in baked breads and cakes. The fresh or dried petals can be softened in milk and added to cake, bread and biscuit recipes. Dried petals can also be stored for use in the winter.

Marigolds make a soothing healer for sore skin and slight wounds, and they can be infused to make a lotion for sunburn. It is claimed that a tisane made from the petals is good for the complexion and the circulation. As this herb has always been connected with treating the skin, here is a simple recipe for a fruity face pack to freshen and soften the face.

Peach & marigold face pack

1 fresh peach
10 marigold flower heads
Almonds, ground

Pick the petals from each flower head and put into a food processor. Peel the peach and slice into small pieces. Add the peach to the petals and process quickly. Stir in enough ground almonds to make a thick paste. Leave for 20 minutes before smoothing on clean skin. Leave on the skin for 15 minutes, then wash off with warm water and pat your face dry. This is an excellent remedy for skin irritated by fierce sun and wind. Keep any extra mixture in the refrigerator for 1 or 2 days.

THE HEALING PROPERTIES OF MARIGOLD PETALS HAVE LONG BEEN EXPLOITED. HERE, THE PETALS COMBINE WITH A FRESH PEACH TO MAKE A SOOTHING FACE MASK.

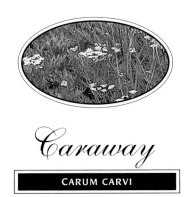

Caraway

CARUM CARVI

Caraway is another herb from the large umbellifer family. It is grown chiefly for its seeds, which are most often used in food and drinks. It is a biennial plant with soft, feathery leaves, and it grows as high as 2 feet (60 cm). In its second year, caraway produces masses of small, white flowers which become little fruits. When ripe, the fruits burst open to reveal two crescent-shaped seeds with a delicious and distinctive flavour. The root, which is long and resembles a carrot, has the same flavour and is sometimes eaten as a vegetable. The leaves, though not in popular use, may be included in raw salads. Most of the seed bought commercially comes from Holland, but a small amount is still grown in Britain.

Caraway is best sown from seed late in the summer to produce flowers the following year. It does need to be in a position where it will get enough sun to ripen the seed. When the seed heads are ripe, cut the stem at ground level and place it in a paper bag to catch the seeds as they fall. Store seeds in airtight containers.

Goosnargh cakes

MAKES ABOUT 20 CAKES

8 oz (225 g) plain flour
Pinch of salt
1 heaped teaspoon caraway seeds
6 oz (175 g) butter
Caster sugar, to coat

Mix together the flour, salt and caraway seeds, then rub in the butter. Knead to a smooth dough. Roll out to about ¼ inch (0.5 cm) thick. Cut the dough into small rounds and dredge with sugar. Place on a greased baking sheet and leave overnight. Bake in a cool oven at 130°C (250°F) Mark ½ for 30–45 minutes until the cakes are firm but not brown. While warm, sift on a little more sugar.

GOOSNARGH CAKES HAVE A STRONG CARAWAY FLAVOUR.

THESE SAVOURY
BISCUITS ARE MADE
WITH ROQUEFORT
CHEESE AND
CARAWAY SEEDS,
AND ARE BEST
SERVED WITH
SHERRY OR
COCKTAILS AS AN
HORS-D'OEUVRE.

At one time caraway was frequently used with many foods, and was made into little sweets called comfits, which were thought to strengthen the eyesight. Today there are few British recipes using the seeds, however they are commonly used in Jewish and European cookery. Kümmel is the German name for caraway and is also the name for a liqueur based on the flavour. Rye breads often have caraway included, and the seeds are successfully added to hearty winter dishes of cabbage and beetroot. The seeds may also be used in cheeses, soups and stews. However, the flavour turns bitter with long cooking, so it is best to add caraway near the end of the cooking method. One traditional British recipe from the Midlands is for little, rich biscuits called Goosnargh cakes. A plain cake flavoured with caraway was also a regular feature of Victorian tea-times.

Roquefort & caraway biscuits

•

M·A·K·E·S A·B·O·U·T 24 B·I·S·C·U·I·T·S

This savoury biscuit is best served with an aperitif.

3½ oz (100 g) butter
4 oz (110 g) plain flour
3 oz (75 g) Roquefort cheese, crumbled
2 teaspoons caraway seeds
Pepper

Preheat oven to 220°C (425°F) Mark 7. Rub the butter into the flour and mix in cheese. Add the caraway seeds and a good grinding of pepper. Form small balls from the mixture and place on a baking sheet, flattening them slightly. Bake for 8–10 minutes. Remove to a wire rack to cool.

Feverfew

CHRYSANTHEMUM PARTHENIUM

Today feverfew is mainly grown for its decorative qualities rather than its medicinal properties, though in the past few years it has become popular as a herbal remedy for migraine and various other ailments. The name feverfew suggests that it was once known as a cure for illnesses, but in old herbals it is sometimes known as featherfew, perhaps to describe the delicately cut, pretty leaves. It is also called the febrifuge plant.

Feverfew has become naturalized in many parts of the world, but is probably a native of south-eastern Europe. It is a bushy, hardy perennial, but usually grown as an annual. Feverfew reproduces rapidly, and one plant will spread seedlings far and wide, but they are easy to remove. Often the seedlings settle in a perfect spot and are best left to flourish. The whole plant has a pungent scent, not unlike that of chamomile, and the taste of the leaves is strong and bitter.

The common form of feverfew has bright green leaves and small, white, yellow-centred flowers on branching stems. It grows to about 15 inches (38 cm) tall. There is also a golden-leaved version known as 'Aureum' which is delightful in a mixed flower border or among herbs in a herb garden where the plant has a light and sunny effect. A double-flowered variety is also available and it is a popular plant for cottage gardens. All types are attractive simply in leaf early in the year when the plant forms a compact, rounded bush. Later during the summer, it becomes more open and spreading and the white flowers appear.

In Victorian times, feverfew plants were often used in elaborate, formal bedding schemes of summer flowers where they provided excellent foliage colour and were easy and well-behaved plants to grow. In addition to flower beds and herb gardens, feverfew is also attractive in pots on a patio or in window-boxes.

Buy small plants to replant straight into the garden, or sow feverfew seed early in the year in gentle heat or later, in spring, out of doors. Transplant the small seedlings to give them more space and put them into their final positions in early summer. They are happy in a variety of soils, and thrive in sun or partial shade. They do, however, seem to need plenty of moisture.

Stems of flowering feverfew last well in water when brought indoors and are a useful addition to summer flower arrangements. They add a natural freshness when mixed with other flowers or when just used alone. They do not need any special treatment, except checking that the water is fresh after a few days. Bear in mind that the container will have to be quite small, as the stems cannot be picked with much length.

TIDY WHITE AND YELLOW FEVERFEW FLOWERS ARE EXCELLENT AS CUT FLOWERS, WORKING WELL ALONE IN SMALL BUNCHES, AS HERE, OR MIXED WITH OTHER HERBS AND FLOWERS.

WITH ITS SMALL FLOWERS AND COMPACT GROWTH, FEVERFEW MAKES A PLEASANTLY ATTRACTIVE ADDITION TO ALL TYPES OF GARDENS.

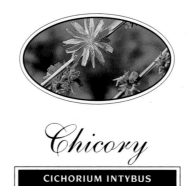

Chicory

CICHORIUM INTYBUS

Many different types of plants are known as chicory. Unfortunately, the European names are often different from the British names. The fact that the plant is used for forcing as a winter vegetable, as well as for a salad leaf, leads to further confusion. The wild chicory still found growing along roadsides and in wastelands is *Cichorium intybus*, and it is a hardy perennial grown throughout Europe and North America. It is sometimes calles succory or wild succory. The erect, branched stems grow to about 3 feet (90 cm) and have beautiful, sky blue or violet-blue flowers which are similar to dandelion. There is also a pink-flowered variety. The flowers add a lovely touch to natural flower arrangements.

Traditionally the roots have been used dried and ground as a substitute for coffee. The varieties bred from this type of chicory can be forced to provide the fat, solid, white chicons, or hearts, which are sold commercially as chicory or Belgian chicory and which provide the delicious bitter salad ingredient.

Another chicory plant, *Cichorium endivia,* has many cultivars commonly known as endive. The French call them frisée or escarole. These are a range of leafy plants, some red-streaked and some frilly-edged, which make delicious salads throughout the year. In Italy, all chicories are known as radicchio, but in Britain only the red varieties are known under this name.

For any gardener interested in producing fresh salad crops throughout the year, the enormous chicory and endive families are worth exploring. Many are very easy to grow, and once cut will reappear again. The plants can also be eaten when small, and then seeds should be sown regularly. Some of the most useful are the sugar loaf chicories, which produce large, cos, lettuce-type plants during the autumn and early winter when other leafy vegetables are scarce. Some types have decoratively cut leaves.

To reduce the bitterness of the green leaf, the whole plant is often blanched for a few days. This is done by covering the plant's leaves to exclude all light, which has the effect of turning the leaves a pale creamy colour and increasing bitterness in the taste.

The forced white chicons are often used in cooked dishes as well as in raw salads, but most of the leafy types are made into raw dishes. A few leaves of slightly bitter chicory added to mixed greens of lettuce and other leaves greatly improves the flavour of a salad. One classic and popular salad recipe is made from crisp, white chicory leaves and fresh oranges.

SKY BLUE CHICORY FLOWERS HAVE A SHORT LIFE-SPAN, BUT MAKE LOVELY ARRANGEMENTS. HERE, THEY ARE MIXED WITH SCENTED SWEET PEAS AND BLUE CORNFLOWERS.

CHICORY ADDS A BITTERNESS TO LEAFY SALADS, WHICH ENLIVENS THE TASTE DRAMATICALLY. THE BLUE FLOWERS ALSO ENHANCE THE COLOUR OF THE SALAD.

Mixed chicory salad

•

SERVES 6—8

This salad can be made at all times of the year, but the blue flowers will only be in season during the summer and early autumn months.

1 small head oak leaf lettuce
1 small head green cos lettuce
A few leaves of frisée
1 head Belgian chicory
1 small head red radicchio
A few chicory flowers (optional)
Honey vinaigrette (see right)

Wash and carefully dry all the leaves and pull the Belgian chicory apart into individual leaves. Arrange all the leaves in a large salad bowl and dress with the honey vinaigrette.

HONEY VINAIGRETTE

1 tablespoon lemon juice
1 dessert spoon clear honey
1 teaspoon prepared French mustard
Salt and pepper
3 tablespoons olive oil

Mix lemon juice, honey, mustard and seasonings together, then slowly add the oil, stirring constantly. Alternatively, shake all the ingredients in a screw-top jar.

Coriander

CORIANDRUM SATIVUM

Coriander is an intriguing herb, as it is one of the few herbs used as a fresh leaf and as a dried seed. The green leaves look like a coarser version of flat-leaved parsley and their flavour is unusual and distinctive. Once tried, many people become passionately fond of the herb.

Coriander is probably a native plant of the eastern Mediterranean, along the shores of the Bosphorus and the Dardanelles. It has been used for centuries as both a medicinal and a culinary herb. Today, the aromatic seeds are crushed or ground for use in both sweet and savoury dishes. The seeds are necessary ingredients in many Eastern spice mixtures, and coriander is one of the most common herbs seen for sale in markets from the Middle East to the Far East.

Leeks with coriander sauce

SERVES 4 — 6

1 lb (450 g) baby leeks, trimmed and cleaned
4 tablespoons olive oil
1 tablespoon wine vinegar
Salt and pepper
2 tablespoons sour cream
2 tablespoons thick yoghurt
2 tablespoons mayonnaise
2 tablespoons finely chopped, fresh coriander leaves

Steam or boil the leeks for about 12 minutes, until tender. Drain well and arrange on a flat dish. While still warm, dress the leeks with the oil and vinegar mixed together with a pinch of salt, and pepper. Leave to cool. Just before serving, whisk sour cream, yoghurt and mayonnaise together and mix in chopped coriander. Pour the sauce over leeks and decorate with a few whole coriander leaves.

CORIANDER LEAVES ADD A SPICY FLAVOUR TO THE CREAMY DRESSING FOR THIS BABY LEEK SALAD.

THIS WONDERFULLY FRESH CHUTNEY IS MADE FROM CHOPPED CORIANDER, CHILLI AND GARLIC, AND IS HIGH IN VITAMINS. IT IS BEST SERVED WITH SPICY FOODS.

In North and South America, coriander has been cultivated for thousands of years and is still the most popular herb for many regional dishes. In Europe, it has only begun to make a regular appearance in the last few years.

In most countries, just the leaves of the plant are used, but in India the stalks flavour stocks and soups and in Thailand the roots are pounded into curry pastes. The raw leaf can be scattered over finished dishes, sauces or dips. However, its flavour is robust enough to use with other herbs and spices, and it withstands long cooking.

Coriander is lavishly used in Indian cooking, especially in a fresh, piquant chutney made from the chopped leaves, spices and seasonings. This type of chutney is usually eaten in small amounts as a relish with other foods. It may also be used like a dip for snacks, such as samosas.

Coriander chutney

—————— • ——————

SERVES 6 — 8

½ teaspoon cumin seeds
2 oz (50 g) fresh coriander leaves
½ fresh green chilli, seeded and chopped
1 tablespoon fresh lemon juice
Salt and pepper

Dry-fry the cumin seeds until toasted, then cool them and grind finely. Put the coriander leaves in a food processor or liquidizer. (The liquidizer will produce a smoother result.) Add the remaining ingredients and blend well until smooth. The final mixture is a brilliant green paste. Serve in a small bowl with other Indian dishes and breads.

It is possible to grow coriander for use as a fresh herb, though seed is generally sold for growing plants to produce ripe seeds for storing. Seed merchants do not usually sell named types, but look for coriander described as cilantro or Chinese parsley if you want to grow plants for leaf production. If you want to produce coriander seeds to store, choose varieties from Morocco which are quick to bolt and have minimal leaf.

Coriander is an annual plant, but will withstand quite low temperatures and light frosts, so in some mild climates it will stand over winter. It prefers a light, free-draining soil in a sunny position. The leaf is at its best during the cooler months, while in hotter periods the small pinkish flowers and, later, seeds are produced.

Seeds can be sown indoors and then the seedlings transplanted outside in position, or they can be sown straight into the garden where they are to grow. For a constant supply of the herb, it is sensible to sow coriander seed in succession over a long period. If you have any trouble with seeds germinating, check that the round outer case enclosing the seeds is cracked or shed so moisture can enter and germination can begin.

The leaves of the coriander plant can be harvested as soon as they are big enough to be useful, but when left to flower and seed, a plant can grow up to 2 feet (60 cm) tall. Uproot any plants which are finished, because a plant left to mature will scatter seed all round it and these seedlings can become a nuisance.

Seeds should be harvested when they have turned a greyish brown and feel dry. They will also develop the distinctive coriander aroma, which only happens when the seeds are ripe. Hang bunches of the seed heads loosely inside a paper bag, letting air circulate freely. Leave the bunches in a dry, airy place for several days. When the seeds feel dry, shake them out into the bags and sort through them, choosing the best ones to pack into airtight storage jars.

The flavour of coriander seeds is warm and aromatic with a slight hint of orange in it. Traditionally, coriander seeds are used as spices in pickling. They always appear in the method of cooking called *à la Greque,* in which vegetables or mushrooms are cooked and marinated in a spiced vinegar sauce. In the following recipe, pears are preserved in a spiced pickle and are excellent eaten with cold meats and game, and particularly with cold ham. You will need some large, strong preserving jars with fastenings. The whole spices in the jars are very decorative, but you might prefer to tie them in muslin during cooking and remove them before potting the fruit.

Spiced pickled pears

•

2 lb (900 g) firm pears
1 lb (450 g) sugar
½ pint (300 ml) wine vinegar
8 whole cloves
4 small pieces of cinnamon stick
1 teaspoon whole allspice
2 teaspoons whole coriander seeds

Peel the pears, leaving them whole and the stalk intact. Keep them in acidulated water while you prepare them to prevent discoloration. Measure the sugar and vinegar into a large saucepan and add the spices. Stir over a low heat until sugar has dissolved. Add the pears and bring to the boil. Simmer gently until the pears are just tender. Lift pears out of the syrup and drain. Do not discard the syrup. Pack the pears into sterilized and sealable preserving jars.

Return the saucepan of syrup to the heat and boil until it has been somewhat reduced and is thick. Pour the hot syrup over pears and seal the lids. Store for about 4 weeks before eating.

THE WARM, AROMATIC SCENT OF CORIANDER SEED IS USED TO FLAVOUR THESE SPICED PICKLED PEARS. SERVE THE FRUIT WITH COLD MEATS OR CHEESE.

Rocket

ERUCA SATIVA

ROCKET IS ONE OF THE EASIEST SALAD CROPS TO GROW. BY STAGGERING THE SOWING OF SEEDS, LEAF WILL BE AVAILABLE YEAR-ROUND.

In the past few years, this salad herb has become increasingly popular, perhaps because of the interest in Italian cookery in which it is commonly used. The rich, spicy and pungent flavour of rocket is unlike any other leaf, and the plant is a useful ingredient to enhance plain salads at any time of the year.

Rocket is an annual plant, and is native to countries along the Mediterranean, however it is also naturalized in parts of North America. Originally, its name derived from the Latin *eruca*. From *ruca,* came the name *rochetta* in Old Italian, and then *roquette* in Middle French and rocket in English. The plant may be found under other common names, such as rucola, arugula or rocket salad.

It is an easy plant to grow in the garden or in a window-box, and can be sown from late winter to autumn for an almost year-round supply. Only a small patch of seed needs to be sown at one time, and the plant grows quickly. The large basal leaves should always be eaten when they are young and fresh. Do not use them when they are old and coarse. Any good, fertile soil suits rocket and, though it prefers sunny conditions, it is happy growing in most situations. Hot and dry weather can make the leaves grow tough and peppery, so, ideally, grow a crop for the spring and autumn months when the more common fresh salad ingredients are less available.

The Italians use rocket combined with Parmesan cheese, and the slight sweetness of the cheese offsets the rich flavour of the rocket. Raw mushrooms and cooked or raw beans also work well with the spicy flavour. Heat will destroy the peppery taste of the leaves, but there are many Italian recipes which include blanched rocket leaves with pasta or with other vegetables in cooked dishes.

A good way to introduce yourself to rocket is to make a simple salad with a small amount of the leaves. Combine the leaves with some lettuce and a few shavings of Parmesan, and dress the salad with an olive oil dressing. If you are feeling more adventurous, try the recipes here, or create one of your own.

THE UNUSUAL TASTE OF ROCKET MAKES THE HERB A UNIQUE ADDITION TO MIXED LEAF SALADS OR SPECIAL SALADS, SUCH AS THIS ONE WITH FETA CHEESE AND CROÛTONS.

Feta & rocket salad
·

Choose fresh, young rocket leaves and gently rinse them. Place in a salad bowl and add cubes of feta cheese. Using thick slices of wholemeal or white bread, cube bread into bite-sized chunks. Fry the bread cubes in olive oil until golden and add them to the bowl. This type of salad should be sparsely dressed with a simple lemon juice and olive oil dressing.

Bean & rocket salad
·

SERVES 4

7 oz (200 g) dried white cannellini beans
1 onion
1 carrot
1 stick celery
1 bay leaf
1 garlic clove, crushed
Vinaigrette dressing made from white wine vinegar,
    olive oil and a little French mustard to taste
3 ripe tomatoes, skinned
A bunch of young, fresh rocket leaves, chopped

Soak the beans in water overnight or for several hours. Discard the water and put the beans in a large pan with the onion, carrot, celery and bay leaf. Just cover with water and bring to the boil. Boil for 10 minutes, then simmer 30–40 minutes, until the beans are cooked. Drain the beans and remove vegetables. Add the crushed garlic to the vinaigrette dressing.

Chop the tomato flesh into small pieces and add to the beans. Pour a little vinaigrette over the warm beans and mix well. Leave until cool, then add in the chopped rocket leaves. Do not refrigerate this dish, as the cold spoils the flavours. Serve with crusty bread as a starter or for part of a main meal.

Fennel

FOENICULUM VULGARE

Fennel is a perennial herb found wild along the Mediterranean, but it is also cultivated throughout Europe and North America. Historically, the herb was used medicinally; the ancient Greeks believed that it induced courage and provided stamina. In the Middle Ages in Europe, fennel seeds were used to stave off hunger during long religious fasts and, in more recent times, the seeds became known as 'meetin' seeds' by chapelgoers in early America, who chewed the seeds during long and tedious sermons.

Fennel is a tall, graceful, perennial plant and grows up to 5–6 feet (1.5–2 m) high. The leaves are finely dissected and similar to dill leaves in appearance, though the two herbs differ in taste. Fennel usually has bright green leaves which mature to a darker green later in the season, but there is also a variety with bronze leaves. The young leaves of the bronze variety are a smoky pink-purple at first, and later become bronze. Both types of fennel produce large umbels of yellow flowers. Removing the flower heads periodically helps keep the plant living longer; however, you may want to keep the flowers, in order to produce seed for sowing or drying.

Fennel grows easily from seed, but it is also possible to buy young plants for planting out into position. Soil conditions are not very important for the plant, but plants will grow larger if they are given a rich humus soil. Choose a sunny site, if possible.

Both fennel leaves and seeds are used in cooking to add a distinctive sweet and anise flavour. Fennel seeds are often dried, and they have a stronger flavour than the soft, feathery leaves. The seeds appear in many cuisines throughout the world, from Scandinavian pickled foods to Indian curries. They are sometimes used in breads, cakes, with fruit tarts, or in tea.

Fennel leaves are suitable for using in soups, salads or with pork or veal. The most popular way to use the leaves is with fish, either in a sauce recipe or directly on a barbecue. During the summer, pick a few whole stems of fennel to dry; remove the leaves and make small bunches of the hollow stems. Hang them to dry in a warm, dry place, then store in an airy, but cool, place. A few stems tossed on to the burning charcoal of a barbecue creates an enchanting aroma and subtly flavours the fish cooking above.

THE FLOWER HEADS OF FENNEL ARE LARGE AND SPECTACULAR. IF THEY ARE LEFT TO SET SEED, COLLECT THE SEEDS AND DRY THEM FOR USE AS A FLAVOURING.

Barbecued red mullet with fennel

·

SERVES 4

A large bunch of fresh fennel
4 fresh red mullet, cleaned and scaled,
    with fins and gills removed
Juice of 1 lemon
Olive oil
Salt and pepper
Lemon slices and chopped fennel leaves, to garnish

Strip the leaves from the fennel stems and chop finely. Chop the smaller stems very finely, and use the large, tough stems to burn on the barbecue while cooking.

Ensure each fish is rinsed thoroughly. Pat dry with absorbent kitchen paper. Stuff the cavity of each fish with the chopped fennel leaves and stems. Using three quarters of the lemon juice, pour a little juice inside each cavity. Brush the outside of the fish with olive oil. Sprinkle the remaining lemon juice over the skin of the fish. Season each fish with salt and pepper and grill over a hot barbecue for 5–10 minutes on each side, until the flesh is cooked and the skin is slightly brown. Garnish with lemon slices and chopped fennel leaves.

ONE CLASSIC USE OF FENNEL IS WITH FISH. HERE, RED MULLET IS STUFFED WITH FRESH FENNEL AND GRILLED OUTDOORS OVER FENNEL STEMS.

THE SOFT,
FEATHERY LEAVES
OF FLORENCE
FENNEL MAKE A
HIGHLY DECORATIVE
ADDITION TO THE
HERB OR
VEGETABLE GARDEN
IN LATE SUMMER.

Florence fennel is related to the ordinary fennel, but it is an annual. It is known botanically as *Foeniculum vulgare dulce* and by the common name, finocchio. It is similar in appearance to the fennel herb, however it has a swollen base to the stem. This bulb makes a delicious vegetable and can be cooked or used raw. The leaves and seeds can be used in the same way as those of the fennel herb, however the leaves may have slightly less flavour.

Florence fennel can be difficult to grow in cooler climates, as it requires a hot summer season. Choose seed of a variety that is not prone to bolting, and then delay sowing the seed until late spring or early summer. The plant needs well-drained, moist soil, and it should be grown quickly to keep the stems young and tender. Though it likes a warm climate, in dry weather the bulbs may not swell, but become stringy or simply bolt to seed. Thin out the seedlings and keep them well watered to encourage growth. The bulb will swell and sit on top of the soil, anchored by a long tap root. Harvest the bulbs when they have reached a good size, but before they produce flower stems.

The clean anise taste of the raw Florence fennel bulb is refreshing and sweet. The bulb is perfect for crunchy salads, and the flavour combines well with other ingredients, such as apples, oranges, potatoes and tomatoes. In Italy, the fennel bulb is often eaten after a meal to cleanse the palate. The Italians have a large repertoire of recipes for using Florence fennel, as it is a well-loved vegetable in Italy.

One idea for using the fennel bulb is to dip small pieces of chopped raw Florence fennel into a light batter and deep-fry the pieces. Serve the fried fennel very hot with lemon wedges. Baked fennel is another delicious recipe; the flavour of the herb becomes mild and the texture quite soft.

Braised fennel with Parmesan

•

SERVES 4

The fine flavour of baked fennel is accentuated in this simple recipe. Serve it as an accompaniment to fish or chicken dishes, or serve it alone as a starter.

4 Florence fennel bulbs
1 lemon, sliced
Salt and pepper
Butter
1 garlic clove, crushed
Juice of 1 lemon
Parmesan cheese, freshly grated

Cut off the feathery green tops and the base of each fennel bulb. Discard any tough outer layers. Slice the bulbs vertically from top to bottom in 2 or 3 pieces.

Place the bulbs in a saucepan and cover with water. Add salt and the lemon slices. Simmer for 15 minutes until the fennel feels tender, then remove from the heat and drain.

Layer the fennel in a large, shallow, ovenproof dish, scattering salt, pepper and dots of butter between the layers. Add the crushed garlic clove and sprinkle with lemon juice. Top with enough grated Parmesan to make a thin coating over the dish. Cover with aluminium foil and bake in the oven at 190°C (375°F) Mark 5 for 20 minutes. Remove the foil and increase the oven temperature to 220°C (425°F) Mark 7 for a further 15 minutes, until the cheese is brown and bubbling. Remove and serve.

ITALIAN CUISINE IS
RICH WITH RECIPES
USING FLORENCE
FENNEL, AND ONE
POPULAR DISH IS
THIS BRAISED
FENNEL WITH
PARMESAN CHEESE.

Hyssop

HYSSOPUS OFFICINALIS

Hyssop is a pretty, shrubby perennial, native to southern Europe, but it has been introduced into Britain and the warmer regions of the United States. It is mainly used as a decorative plant in the garden, where it makes neat, low edgings of narrow, dark green leaves. The leaves become smothered in deep purplish blue, hooded flowers in late summer when many other herbs have finished flowering. The flowers bloom along curving, tall, hairy stems which need to be cut down after flowering has occurred. There are varieties with pink, white or pale blue flowers. Insects and honey bees love the flowers, so hyssop is necessary for anyone with a hive of bees to feed.

The plants become quite woody and thick, and they are excellent grown into a low hedge or path edging where they can be kept neat with a little light clipping.

At one time, hyssop was used medicinally, especially in treatments for coughs and catarrh. A hot tisane, made from hyssop leaves, is particularly good for combating colds and relieving painful sinuses. The ancient Romans made a wine using the leaves and, from medieval to Elizabethan times in Britain, hyssop was included among the 'strewing herbs', a scented mixture which was used to cover and protect the floor and sweeten the room.

Hyssop can be grown from seed, but it is easier to buy small plants in containers from nurseries to plant out into position. Choose a sunny and well-drained site in the garden, and leave 2 feet (60 cm) of space between each plant. To increase stock, you can take stem cuttings in the spring, or else divide established plants in autumn or early spring. Hyssop plants will last for many years, but, like many small shrubby plants, they will eventually lose their vigour and may need replacing. Hyssop deserves to be better known, and more often grown, as it is easy to cultivate, pretty, and brings a welcome patch of deep blue to a flower border.

The flavour of hyssop is slightly bitter, minty and strong, so it is used in small quantities as a flavouring for sweet and savoury foods. The highly decorative flowers can be used as an edible garnish. Hyssop is delicious in stuffings, especially ones to accompany rich meats, and it is good with pork. It also combines well with fruit dishes. The renowned French liqueur, chartreuse, includes hyssop as one of its flavouring herbs.

A SIMPLE PINK AND YELLOW GRAPEFRUIT SALAD IS MADE INTO AN ELEGANT DISH WITH THE ADDITION OF A SUBTLE HYSSOP-FLAVOURED SYRUP.

THE PURPLE-BLUE FLOWERS OF HYSSOP BLOOM LATE IN THE SUMMER AND ARE EXCEPTIONALLY ATTRACTIVE TO HONEY BEES.

Grapefruit salad with hyssop syrup

SERVES 4—6

This recipe makes a superb breakfast dish. It also makes an excellent starter or dessert for a meal in which the main course is rich.

2 large pink grapefruit, peeled
2 large yellow grapefruit, peeled
2 tablespoons granulated sugar
2 tablespoons water
2 sprigs hyssop leaves
Juice of 1 lemon
A few hyssop flowers and leaves, to decorate

Remove segments from the grapefruit by cutting each segment close to the membrane and lifting out the segment. Once the segments have been removed, place them on a plate and squeeze any juice from the membrane over the fruit.

Dissolve the sugar in the water and bring to the boil. Simmer for a few minutes, then add in the hyssop leaves and reduce heat. Leave to cool. Add the lemon juice to the syrup, then strain to remove the leaves.

Arrange the grapefruit segments in individual fruit bowls or in one large bowl. Pour over the syrup and chill. Decorate the fruit with hyssop flowers and a sprig of hyssop leaf.

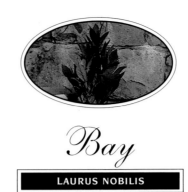

Bay

LAURUS NOBILIS

The bay leaf is an ancient and noble herb. For the ancient Greeks, the bay, or laurel, leaf was an emblem of glory, and the herb was twined into wreaths or crowns to be worn by the victorious. Laurel wreaths were awarded as a sign of achievement, and athletes and poets as well as statesmen were often the recipients. The herb is also commonly called bay laurel, bay tree, sweet bay, Roman laurel or Grecian laurel. According to ancient folklore, a bay tree growing in the garden will keep away evil, witches, and thunder and lightning.

Notwithstanding these doubtful properties, a bay tree is a lovely evergreen plant to own. The plant is vigorous, reaching 30 feet (9 m) or more, if allowed to grow. It can also be clipped and contained in a small pot. In fact, bay trees are most often seen as small, decorative, formal bushes trained into standards on a long, single stem, or cut into spirals or cones.

The tough, dark green leaves are sweetly aromatic. This is the part of the plant which is used as a herb, though the creamy white flowers, the small purple berries and the reddish brown stems are all aromatic. The stature of a full-grown bay tree is certainly impressive. It is probably the largest shrub grown in the Northern Hemisphere for herbal and culinary uses. It is the only member of the *Laurus* genus that is used in cooking.

Bay thrives in sun, but will tolerate coastal conditions. However, the plant can suffer from severe winter weather. If all the leaves are damaged, the plant will often re-sprout leaves from the base. Propagation is not very easy, so it is often best to buy a small plant if you want to grow one in a container or garden. Cuttings can be taken from the stem in late summer, or, sometimes, the low branches can be layered into the ground beside the main plant. Occasionally, a large and mature bush will conveniently sow dozens of seedlings at its base; these seedlings can then be potted up. Bay is slow to grow, compared with most herbs, but it is a good long-term investment.

Bay is most often used to flavour stocks, stews, sauces and other dishes by including it in a bouquet garni. This little posy of herbs, either tied together or encased in a muslin bag, is added to many dishes to give a subtle lift of flavour. The bouquet garni is always removed at the end of the cooking method.

BAY PLANTS FLOURISH IN POTS AND ALWAYS LOOK DECORATIVE. THEY WILL WITHSTAND QUITE SEVERE CLIPPING TO KEEP THEM IN SHAPE.

Bouquet garni

———— • ————

MAKES 1

*Fresh herbs are preferable, but you may substitute dried herbs, except for parsley,
which should always be used fresh.*

1 bay leaf
1 sprig thyme
1 sprig fresh parsley
A small piece celery stick
A piece of thread or string

Make a small bunch from all the herbs in your hands, then tie them tightly round the stems with the thread or string. For an average amount of food or liquid, 1 bay leaf is usually sufficient, as the flavour is very strong.

A BOUQUET GARNI SHOULD ALWAYS INCLUDE A BAY LEAF OR TWO. IF YOU DO NOT HAVE FRESH LEAVES, DRIED LEAVES CAN BE SUBSTITUTED.

Fresh bay leaves are more desirable than dry, and they can be gathered throughout the whole year; if you own a bay tree you will not need to dry bay for storing. However, bay does dry well and keeps its fragrance better than many other herbs. To dry some leaves, either pick small branches of bay and dry the branches whole, or strip off individual leaves from the stem and press them flat. On drying, the leaves will naturally curl and eventually become very brittle. Once dried, they should be stored away from the light.

The bay leaf is a classic French cooking herb which, in addition to flavouring soup stocks, is used to flavour meat, fish, poultry and vegetables. Bay leaves are excellent in marinade mixtures to flavour and tenderize meat. They are an important ingredient in Greek-style skewered grilled meats, such as lamb or fish. Savoury white sauces, such as béchamel, are improved by using milk infused with a bay leaf. A unique way to use bay is the old-fashioned English idea of using it as a flavouring for sweet dishes, particularly milk-based puddings, such as rice pudding or custards. The warm, slightly spicy taste of the bay leaves works beautifully with the mild smoothness of creamy desserts.

Individual bay custards

SERVES 4

These delicate baked custards are best eaten cold, but not over-chilled. You may like to serve them with poached fruit or with a thin pouring of single cream.

¾ pint (450 ml) milk
4 fresh bay leaves (dried, if fresh are not available)
3 eggs
1 oz (25 g) granulated sugar
Fresh bay leaves, to decorate

In a saucepan, gently heat the milk with the bay leaves until the liquid reaches the boiling point. Then remove from the heat and leave to infuse for about 10 minutes.

Beat the eggs and sugar together until light and fluffy. Strain the infused milk and pour on to the egg mixture. Stir well. Strain into 4 individual ramekin dishes. Place the ramekins on a deep-sided baking tray containing 1 inch (2.5 cm) of water. Bake in the oven at 140°C (275°F) Mark 1 for about 1½ hours until set. Remove from the oven, cool, and decorate.

THIS UNUSUAL VERSION OF OLD-FASHIONED BAKED CUSTARD IS DELICATELY FLAVOURED WITH BAY LEAVES.

FOOD COOKED ON
SKEWERS ALWAYS
BENEFITS FROM A
MARINADE FIRST TO
FLAVOUR AND
TENDERIZE. FRESH
BAY LEAVES ARE
ESSENTIAL FOR THIS
RECIPE.

Monkfish kebabs with lime & bay marinade

SERVES 4

Monkfish is ideal for this recipe, as the flesh is firm and solid. If you do not have monkfish, substitute swordfish, tuna or a white fish, such as haddock or cod.

1 lb (450 g) monkfish, skinned and with membrane removed
3 whole garlic cloves, peeled
Marinade (see below right)
A bunch of fresh bay leaves
1 lime, sliced

Cut the fish into bite-sized cubes. Chop each garlic clove into 2 or 3 pieces.

Lay the cubed fish in a large shallow dish and pour over the marinade. Tuck in, among the fish pieces, the bay leaves, lime slices and garlic pieces. Cover with cling film and leave in a cool place for at least 1 hour for the flavour to absorb into the fish.

Prepare a hot grill or barbecue. When it is ready, thread fish on to skewers, alternating with bay leaves and lime slices. Brush with the marinade and cook over the grill for 3–5 minutes each side, turning frequently, and brushing with more marinade until the fish is opaque and tender.

MARINADE

Juice of 1 lime
¼ pint (150 ml) olive oil
Salt and pepper

To make the marinade, mix the lime juice with the olive oil, and add salt and pepper.

Lavender

LAVANDULA SPICA

Lavender has been grown for centuries for medicinal purposes as well as for decorative and fragrant uses in the home. It is a familiar and well-loved plant, and makes the most beautiful, fragrant, small shrub or path edging for a garden. If you have space, grow at least one bush of lavender near a path or doorway to appreciate the fragrance as you brush against it.

There are over 25 species in the *Lavandula* genus. *Lavandula spica* is also known botanically as *L. angustifolia* and *L. officinalis*, and this is the one most commonly grown. It is native to the Mediterranean regions. French lavender, *L. stoechas*, and Dutch lavender, *L. vera*, are generally more compact plants.

Lavender flowers are usually a beautiful shade of mauve, but there are also varieties with deep purple, white or pink flowers. The plant blooms from the middle of the summer until very early autumn. The stems of the plant are downy and grey-green, and the whole plant grows to about 2–3 feet (60–90 cm) high.

Recently, lavender plants with dwarf characteristics have been developed; these varieties are ideal for growing as low hedges or path edgings. The best scented varieties are the larger, old-fashioned types, such as *Lavandula spica* 'Seal', 'Grappenhall' and 'Old English'.

Ideally, lavender prefers well-drained, slightly sandy soil in a sunny position, though it will survive most situations. However, some of the more tender types do not like very cold weather, and none relish cold, waterlogged soil in winter. Lavender bushes will last for years, but it is best to replace old bushes after five or six years.

As a fresh flower, lavender has great charm and mixes well with other flowers in an arrangement. The soft mauve colour looks lovely with other summer flowers, such as roses, sweet peas and cornflowers. Stems of dried lavender are an excellent addition to dried arrangements, but they often get lost among more sturdy flowers. The best way of using dried lavender stems is to make a simple sheaf or bundle, using only one variety of lavender so the colour is concentrated.

Dried lavender sheaf

If you grow your own lavender, cut it with long stems and hang it in small bunches upside-down in a warm, dark place. When the bunches are fully dry, make a big bunch in your hands, keeping all the flower heads at the same level. Tie the bundle round the stems and cut off the bottom of all the stems to the same length. This arrangement can stand on its own, but, for a different effect, put it in a flower pot or basket.

A TALL, FROSTED GLASS VASE IN A MODERN SHAPE EMPHASIZES THE PRETTINESS OF FRESH, PALE MAUVE LAVENDER.

A SMALL COTTAGE WINDOW MAKES THE PERFECT FRAME FOR A SHEAF OF DRIED, DEEP PURPLE LAVENDER, TIED WITH A SIMPLE BOW.

Lavender's strong, refreshing and astringent scent makes the herb a useful ingredient for scented sachets, pot-pourris, and bath products of all kinds. Infused lavender can be used for soothing and slightly antiseptic lotions, hair rinses, or as a refreshing cold compress for headaches and fatigue. Lavender water is a fragrant and mild refreshener, particularly recommended for sensitive and delicate skin.

Since Roman times, and probably long before, lavender has been used with laundry; clean clothes and linen were laid out over lavender bushes to dry in the sun, and dried lavender stems and flowers were scattered among dried and pressed linen. In fact, the name lavender originated from the Latin *lavare*, meaning 'to wash'. Lavender bags are still used today when storing clothes or fabric for any length of time.

To dry lavender for using in pot-pourri sachets, pick the flower heads when the flowers are fully open and leave them to dry in a warm, dark place. When they are dry, strip the tiny flowers off the stalks and use the dried flowers in a pot-pourri recipe. Or, use the freshly picked stems for making bottles to store with linen. With this method, the flower heads will dry encased inside the lavender stems.

Lavender bottles

To make one bottle, you will need about 20 stems of lavender, freshly picked, and with the flowers fully opened. Tie a thin piece of thread around the base of the flower heads and bend each stem back in turn, encasing the flower heads. When they are all bent back, arrange them neatly and tie together with string or ribbon just beneath the enclosed flowers, weaving in and out of the stems. Leave the bottle to dry naturally before using.

LAVENDER BOTTLES AND POT-POURRI CAN BE DISPLAYED IN OPEN CONTAINERS. THE POT-POURRI SHOWN HERE HAS LARKSPUR AND CORNFLOWERS ADDED TO ENHANCE THE BASIC MIXTURE.

Lavender pot-pourri

•

4 cups dried lavender flowers
1 cup dried blue larkspur
1 cup dried blue cornflowers
¼ cup dried mint leaves
2 tablespoons dried rosemary
2 tablespoons dried orris root, as fixative
6 drops lavender essential oil

Mix all the ingredients together, except the oil. Add oil, drop by drop, mixing thoroughly. Put the mixture into a large paper bag, seal securely, and leave in a warm, dark place for 6 weeks to cure. Occasionally, shake the contents. Display the pot-pourri in shallow dishes and add a few whole dried flower heads on top, if desired.

Home-made lavender water

•

This refreshing herb-scented water is perfect to add to a bath or use as a skin lotion and cooler on a hot day. Keep it in a securely stoppered bottle.

2 cups fresh or dried lavender flowers
1 pint (600 ml) distilled water
2 fl oz (60 ml) vodka
6 drops lavender essential oil

Put the lavender flowers in a jar or bottle. Bring the water to the boil and pour over the flowers. Leave to cool. Add the vodka, and then the lavender oil. Cover the jar or bottle and leave for 2 weeks. Then strain the liquid, pour into pretty bottles, and add a fresh sprig of lavender.

Two hundred years ago, acres of land on the southern edge of London were used to grow lavender on a vast commercial scale. The soil and climate suited the plant well, and some famous and successful companies became world-renowned for their lavender products. The lavender industry in England has now dwindled to one company in Norfolk, and the old lavender fields are now covered by houses. The fragrance of lavender is secreted in oil glands, which are found in the hairs that cover the whole plant. Lavender is distilled by steam to extract the oil.

Other centres of the lavender industry are in the United States and France. In the south of France, and centred round Grasse, the perfume region, lavender is still grown commercially, though not on the scale it once was. This part of France has wild lavender growing throughout the garigue scrub along the Mediterranean shores.

Lavender oil is still an important natural flower oil in the perfume and fragrance industry. Unfortunately, natural fragrances are now secondary to artificial aromas created in laboratories. The appeal of the lavender scent is easy to understand. The smell is fresh, astringent and clean. In fact, it was one of the few perfumes permitted by the Puritans, as it was viewed as a wholesome and homely scent. In folklore, lavender maintains chastity, so this may be the reason it was so appealing to the Puritans.

At one time, lavender was used frequently in the kitchen. Today its culinary use is restricted to flavouring sorbets and syrups. One of the most delicious ways of enjoying lavender in food is to find a source of lavender honey. The taste is subtle and sweet, and the honey is perfect to use as a sweetener for ice-cream and other desserts.

Lavender can be used to flavour a refreshing sorbet based on lemon. Sprigs of fresh lavender can also be infused in the liquid juice in a jelly recipe. Use a lavender-flavoured sugar to make a lavender icing for a light vanilla sponge cake, or, include lavender sugar in a custard sauce, and serve the sauce with a tart or other pastry dessert. Lavender vinegar is a novel addition to a dressing for a salad made from mixed leaves and flowers. However, the lavender scent is likely to get lost if used with highly robust flavours.

Lavender sugar

Collect 2 or 3 spikes of fresh, but slightly dry, lavender. Fill a glass jar with sugar and insert the spikes in the jar. Cover and leave for several weeks for the scent to be absorbed into the sugar. The flavour will be pleasantly subtle.

Lavender vinegar

In a jar, add several lavender flower heads and a sprig of lavender, along with 1 or 2 twists of lemon or orange peel. Fill with a light cider or wine vinegar, seal securely, and leave for several weeks before using.

Cress

LEPIDIUM SATIVUM

There are several different plants which all come under the heading of cress. Some are grown as garden plants, while others are best used as sprouted seeds or when very small (these types can be grown indoors without soil). Cresses of all kinds have long been popular foods, supplying many important minerals and vitamins and providing fresh green leaves to brighten up an often dreary and monotonous diet of preserved food. The Victorians loved the taste of peppery cresses and used them in tea-time sandwiches as well as to decorate dishes for a cold table. During this time period, watercress picked fresh from clear streams was a country favourite to eat with the supper meal of the rural worker, alongside cheese or cold meats.

LITTLE CRESS SEEDLINGS ARE EASY TO GROW INDOORS ON DAMP PAPER OR FABRIC. THEY PROVIDE A REGULAR SUPPLY FOR SALADS AND GARNISHES.

Cress is not usually classified as a herb, but it is used in much the same way that herbs are used – to add zest to food. Normally eaten fresh and raw, and in quite small quantities, cress is enjoying a revival in its popularity. Use it instead of lettuce in sandwiches or salads, or as a garnish for main dishes or hors-d'oeuvres.

For the small sprouted seedlings, which are often sold in little plastic punnets in shops, buy seed of garden cress (*Lepidium sativum*). This plant can be grown in a small patch outdoors, but it is particularly successful sown indoors in a tray on damp paper, fabric, or any growing medium. Spread the seeds evenly on damp paper, pressing down lightly. Water with tepid water and cover with brown paper. When the seeds have germinated, remove the cover and keep moist. It is ready for harvesting as soon as the tiny seedlings have two good-sized leaves, about three or four weeks after sowing.

Commercial punnets often contain a mixture of cress and salad rape (*Brassica napus*) or just rape seedlings, though once the mix was always mustard (*Sinapis alba*) and cress. If you grow your own, experiment with a mixture that suits you until you get a balance you like. When growing cress with mustard or rape, it is often best to sow the cress three days before so that the crops will be ready for harvesting at the same time.

Watercress is known botanically as *Rorippa nasturtium-aquaticum*, *Rorippa microphylla* or *Nasturtium officinale*. It is also commonly known as scurvy grass. At one time watercress was only available through the colder months of the year, but it is now imported to provide a year-round supply. However, the home-grown, dark green-leaved varieties are far superior and are simply bursting with flavour. Watercress soup is a popular and classic recipe which is always successful and worth having in every cook's repertoire.

The leaves of watercress are larger than those of the common cress, and they grow on top of clear, cold, running water, on streams or springs. Watercress can be grown as a garden plant without running water as long as it is grown in moist soil. A better plant to grow in the ground is American or land cress (*Barbarea praecox* or *Barbarea verna*), as it is very hardy and easy to grow, though it should be eaten when young, before it becomes unbearably hot and peppery.

Mixed leaf salad

Choose a range of salad leaves, including different types of lettuce, endive and chicory. Combine them with the same quantity of cresses. If you have a few flower heads of nasturtium, add them too, as they will make a colourful contrast and add a spicy bite.

This salad needs a light and simple dressing so the flavour of the leaves will not be masked. A good dressing would be a vinaigrette made with hazel-nut and sunflower oils, with lemon juice and salt and pepper to taste. Toss the leaves with the vinaigrette dressing in a large bowl and serve the salad immediately.

MIXED GREEN SALADS ARE GIVEN A HOT, PEPPERY BITE AND GOOD TEXTURE WITH THE ADDITION OF CRESSES.

Lovage

LEVISTICUM OFFICINALE

Lovage is a giant plant with a robust flavour to match. In appearance, it is similar to angelica, to which it is related. The stems of lovage are hollow and somewhat like celery stalks. The flavour of the leaves is savoury, with a hint of celery and yeast, and the whole plant is aromatic. Lovage is native to southern Europe and Asia, but it is cultivated in many countries for its use as a culinary herb.

A lovage plant can reach to nearly 7 feet (2 m) if given good, moist soil, so it must be positioned in a garden with care. Like angelica, lovage is a stately and architectural plant best grown on its own in a place where its size can be appreciated.

It should not be hemmed in by other plants nor shading other herbs from the sun.

Lovage should be grown from very fresh seed, and the small plants transplanted into position in late summer. It is a perennial and likely to be healthy for years. Each winter it dies down to soil level and reappears in spring. The first leaves are shiny, deep green, succulent, and mild in flavour. As the season progresses, the leaves become tough and stringy, and the flavour becomes stronger. At this time, typically umbellifer flowers are produced, and they are a yellowish green in colour.

Lovage is a rather old-fashioned herb, and, regrettably, not used as often today as it once was. At one time, the seeds of the plant were infused in liquid to make a medicine to cure digestive illnesses, and the dried seeds were sometimes scattered on the crust of breads before baking. The juice from the plant, or an infusion of the leaves, was used as a treatment to lighten freckles. The stems often candied, in much the same way that angelica is candied today.

Lovage leaves are high in vitamin C and are best used fresh, as they lose most of their flavour when dried. They combine well with spinach, lentils and more bland foods, such as potatoes. Try chopping some young lovage leaves and stems for using in robust salads. If you like the flavour, use the herb more widely. Lovage leaves should always be used fairly sparingly, so they do not dominate other flavours. The taste works well in cold potato salads or with bean salads dressed with a vinaigrette and left to cool. Lovage is a useful herb for stocks, soups and stews, and can be used as a substitute for celery flavouring in many dishes.

HERE ARE A BASKET OF POTATOES AND FRESH LOVAGE LEAVES – PERFECT INGREDIENTS FOR A DELICIOUS SOUP.

THIS SMOOTH AND CREAMY SOUP IS MADE FROM SIMPLE INGREDIENTS. THE STRONG FLAVOUR OF LOVAGE GIVES THE SOUP AN EXCEPTIONAL TASTE.

Lovage & potato soup

SERVES 4—6

This hearty soup is ideal for cool spring days. Serve it with fresh rye bread,
followed by a selection of fruit and cheese.

1 onion, finely chopped
2 oz (50 g) butter
12 oz (350 g) potatoes, peeled and cubed
4 oz (100 g) spinach, washed, drained and chopped
2 oz (50 g) fresh lovage leaves
1¾ pint (1 litre) water or chicken stock
Salt and pepper
Single cream (optional)
Lovage leaves, to garnish

In a large saucepan, soften the onion in the butter over a moderate heat. Add the potatoes and cook for a few minutes longer. Add the spinach and lovage leaves. After a few minutes more, pour in the water or stock. Stir well and simmer uncovered for 30 minutes. Purée the soup in a liquidizer or food processor. Taste, and adjust seasoning. For a richer soup, add a little cream. Float a lovage leaf on each serving.

Lemon Verbena

LIPPIA CITRIODORA

LEMON VERBENA IS BEST GROWN IN POTS INDOORS DURING COLD WINTERS. THE LEAVES OF THE PLANT HAVE A POWERFUL LEMONY SMELL.

Lemon verbena is a shrub from South America. It grows into a small plant with thin, woody stems and long, narrow, pointed leaves, which have the most beautiful lemony scent. The scent is apparent when a leaf is crushed in your fingers. The leaves are most often dried, and used in tisanes or pot-pourri, but can be used to flavour cakes, ice-creams and puddings. The leaves can also be infused to make a mouthwash and cleanser; lemon verbena is said to strengthen teeth and gums as well as prevent tooth decay.

The plant is a perennial shrub, but needs a mild climate to survive. Cold, wet winters and hard frosts will kill even large plants, so, in climates with this sort of weather, the best way to grow lemon verbena is in pots. The potted plant should be kept under cover during the winter, or else in a conservatory or greenhouse throughout the year. In drier, milder areas, the plant can be grown outdoors in a sheltered position. In late summer, the plant produces panicles of tiny, pale mauve or white flowers.

The best time for picking the fresh leaves for drying is during the middle of the summer, when the leaves are still fresh, bright green, and full of scent. Dry the leaves on the stem, or strip them off the stem and dry loose. Store the dried leaves for using in lemon verbena tea or to fill sachets for putting among clothes.

Lemon verbena makes a delightfully fresh and unusual pot-pourri mixture. Many old-fashioned pot-pourri recipes contained lemon verbena, as the leaves added a fresh citrus scent and good green colour, even after drying.

Citrus pot-pourri

2 cups dried lemon verbena leaves

1 cup dried chamomile flowers

1 cup dried spring flowers, such as tulips, daffodils, mimosa, forsythia

Peel of 1 lemon, dried and chopped

Peel of 1 lime, dried and chopped

Peel of 1 grapefruit, dried and chopped

½ cup powdered orris root, as fixative

8 drops lemon verbena essential oil

Long strips of dried lemon or lime peel, or dried flower heads, to decorate

In a large bowl, combine all the ingredients, except the oil. Mix thoroughly. Add the oil in drops and stir well. Pour the mixture into a large paper bag and seal securely. Put the bag in a dark, dry, warm place for 6 weeks to cure, shaking the bag every few days.

Once cured, display the mixture in open bowls or containers, and decorate with dried citrus peel or flower heads. It is always a good idea to save citrus peel throughout the year for using in pot-pourri mixtures.

THIS LEMON-SCENTED POT-POURRI INCLUDES LEMON VERBENA LEAVES, FLOWERS AND CITRUS PEEL, AND IT MAKES A LOVELY YELLOW AND GREEN ASSORTMENT.

Lemon Balm

MELISSA OFFICINALIS

The Latin name of this genus, *Melissa*, derives from the Greek word for bee, and the plant is indeed loved by these insects. Lemon balm has been grown commercially for centuries as a bee plant, and apiarists in the seventeenth century used the plant to contain bees in a hive, particularly when the bees threatened to swarm. Among the many common names for this plant are bee balm, sweet balm, balm mint, blue balm, balm, cure-all and melissa.

Lemon balm is native to the Mediterranean regions, and is often found growing wild in fields or along roadsides. It is cultivated in temperate climates, chiefly for its use as a culinary herb. It is an evergreen perennial, and makes a short bushy plant, about 3 feet (90 cm) high. The numerous stems are branching, hairy, and each one has many toothed, pale green leaves. The insignificant white flowers bloom throughout the summer along the length of stem. From a distance, balm can look very similar to mint.

Lemon balm can be raised from seed, but often takes a long time to germinate. Buying ready-grown plants is an easier way to cultivate balm, or else divide a large plant in the spring and plant out. Lemon balm thrives in ordinary, well-drained soil in the sun, but will also tolerate semi-shady positions. It seeds itself freely, and is difficult to remove once established.

Lemon balm has plain green leaves, but there is also a variegated type, M. *officinalis* 'Aurea', with golden yellow and green leaves. This variety is not quite as vigorous as the species plant, but it can look very pretty planted as a contrast in a herb garden. The gold-green colour may fade as flowering time approaches. Lemon balm leaves dry well and retain their fragrance. Pick leaves for drying just before the flowering season.

HOME-MADE LEMONADE IS A DRINK WELL WORTH THE EFFORT ON HOT SUMMER DAYS, AND IT IS EVEN BETTER WHEN MADE USING LARGE AMOUNTS OF LEMON BALM LEAVES.

The lemon flavour of lemon balm is much more delicate than that of lemon verbena, so it can be used in large quantities for vegetable and fruit salads. A vinaigrette dressing will greatly benefit from a handful of the chopped leaves. The gentle taste of the fresh leaves also combines well with all kinds of fruit, so experiment with the whole leaves as a garnish, or chop the leaves and add to fresh fruit salads or fruit fillings for pies and baked puddings. The leaves are also suitable for using in stuffings, and to flavour jams, jellies and sorbets. They are delicious when used to reinforce the flavour of a lemon mousse.

The fresh leaves are often used for cooling drinks and tisanes. In France, the tea, called melissa tea, is taken as a tonic and remedy for fatigue. In the Middle East, the herb is used to make a fragrant and refreshing hot drink, in much the same way that mint is used. The herb is a wonderful addition to summer fruit punches and wine cups, or home-made lemonade. Both children and adults will enjoy the refreshing taste of lemon balm lemonade, and the drink is authentically sweet rather than over-sweet like many commercial lemonades.

Old-fashioned lemon balm lemonade

MAKES ABOUT 8 GLASSES

4 large juicy lemons, washed and scrubbed
(try to find unwaxed and unsprayed lemons)
5 oz (150 g) granulated sugar
2 pints (1.1 litres) cold water
A bunch of fresh lemon balm leaves
Ice-cubes

Peel the lemons and put the rinds into a heatproof jug. Add the sugar. Pour on just enough boiling water to dissolve the sugar. Then add half the lemon balm leaves. Leave to infuse until cool.

When cool, squeeze the juice from the lemons and add to the syrup. Pour in the cold water to taste, adjusting the sugar or lemon juice to get a good balance. Chill for about 2 hours.
Just before serving, remove the lemon balm and add some more fresh sprigs and ice-cubes. You may also like to remove the lemon peel; if the peel is left in the liquid for too long, it begins to add bitterness.

Mint

MENTHA

Mint must be one of the most widely known and most loved of all the herbs. There are several types within the *Mentha* genus, all with different characteristics. The two most useful culinary mints, and the ones most often grown, are apple or Bowles mint (*Mentha rotundifolia*) and spearmint or garden mint (*Mentha spicata*).

Apple mint has round, soft, pale green, furry leaves and an apple and mint taste, which is sweeter and more subtle than spearmint. Apple mint is resistant to rust disease, which can decimate other varieties. Spearmint is native to the Mediterranean, and has a hot, minty taste and long, narrow, medium green, spear-shaped leaves. This mint was favoured by the Romans who introduced it into northern Europe. Both apple mint and spearmint have spikes bearing purple flowers in summer.

Peppermint (*Mentha piperita*) has a reddish stem and long reddish leaves. It is the most menthol of the mints, and is used predominantly in liqueurs, chocolates and toothpastes. It is this species which is used to produce the true oil of peppermint sold for cooking and medicinal remedies. To produce 8–10 pounds (3.6–4 kg) of oil, 1 ton (1 tonne) of peppermint leaves are needed. The peppermint oil produced by the English is claimed to be a better quality than the oil produced elsewhere.

Other species of mint are pennyroyal (*M. pulegium*), a small-leaved, creeping mint often used dried for tea; ginger mint (*M. x gentilis*) with a spicy scent; Spanish or Corsican mint (*M. requienii*), a tiny variety suitable for growing among paving stones; and eau de cologne mint (*M. citrata*) which has a delicate flavour like oranges or lavender. Water mint (*M. aquatica*) is a rather unpleasant-tasting mint, so it is rarely cultivated. There is also a green and white variegated type known as pineapple mint.

SPEARMINT IS POPULAR FOR ITS HOT, MINTY TASTE. THE LEAVES ARE NARROW AND THE SUMMER FLOWERS ARE PURPLE.

TO ADD A HIGHLY DECORATIVE EFFECT TO YOUR GARDEN, PLANT VARIEGATED MINT ALONG A PATH OR BORDER EDGE.

Many mint varieties are more useful as decorative features to herb gardens rather than as culinary ingredients. All mints, however, are rampant growers. It is often necessary to contain them by planting them in a bottomless bucket in a garden to stop their travelling roots from spreading too far. Another method is to embed slates vertically into the ground round the plant.

Unusually for a herb, mint thrives in moist and dank conditions; in the wild, mint grows at the margins of streams and ponds. Mint is happy in shade or sun, but must have moisture at the roots. It can be grown under a wall or in a shady or difficult bed, but do grow it conveniently near the kitchen so you can use it regularly.

Very few mint varieties come true from seed, and propagation is normally done by taking a small piece of root and growing it into a plant, or by dividing a large plant and transplanting.

HERE, APPLE MINT IS GROWING IN A POT WITH OTHER HERBS. THE DISTINCTIVE LEAVES ARE ROUND AND FURRY, AND HAVE A SWEET APPLE-LIKE TASTE.

There is surprisingly little folklore surrounding mint, which is so commonly used and grown throughout the world. The herb is supposed to symbolize virtue, probably having to do with its clean, fresh scent and astringent properties. For centuries, the refreshing qualities of the herb have been used in tonics and lotions for the skin and hair. The ancient Greeks added mint generously to their bath water. The cooling mint has a long tradition of use in hot countries: mint tea is a speciality of Morocco, and fresh mint and yoghurt is a popular Indian combination, used to accompany highly spiced food. Mint and yoghurt drinks are also popular in the Middle East.

Mint is particularly suited for sweet dishes. It is one of the few herbs which works well with chocolate. A leaf of fresh mint also makes one of the prettiest garnishes. A small sprig is the perfect finishing touch to a cold pudding or a carefully arranged plate of fruit. Use fresh or frosted mint leaves to decorate chocolates, cakes and desserts.

White chocolate & mint mousse

SERVES 4

4 oz (100 g) good-quality white chocolate
8 tablespoons (120 ml) single cream
A bunch of mint leaves
4 eggs, separated
Fresh mint sprigs or frosted mint leaves, to decorate

Carefully melt the chocolate in the top of a double-boiler or in a bowl set over a pan of simmering water. Meanwhile, warm the cream in a small saucepan with about 8 mint leaves. Remove the cream from the heat and leave to infuse for a few minutes.

Stir the egg yolks into the melted chocolate. Whisk the egg whites until stiff. Remove the mint leaves from the cream and add the cream to the chocolate mixture. Stir well, then fold in the egg whites.

Spoon the mousse into small, individual, stemmed glasses and chill for 2–3 hours. Decorate each serving with a sprig of fresh or frosted mint, and serve the mousse as a dessert, with crisp wafers or biscuits.

Sugar-frosted mint leaves

Carefully clean and dry some mint leaves. Brush each leaf on both sides with slightly beaten egg white. Then scatter caster sugar over the surfaces. Place the frosted leaves on a wire rack and leave in a warm place to dry. Other leaves, such as scented geranium leaves, are also suitable for frosting, and mint or geranium leaves are perfectly edible.

Persian yoghurt drink

SERVES 2

5 oz (150 g) plain, unsweetened yoghurt
1/2 pint (300 ml) ice-cold water
Pinch of salt
A small bunch of mint leaves, stripped from the stem
Crushed ice, to serve (optional)

Put the yoghurt and the water in a food processor or liquidizer and blend together until smooth. Add the salt and the mint leaves. Blend again, until the leaves become tiny green specks. Serve with crushed ice, if desired.

Mint tea is a refreshing summer beverage. In the United States, there are several versions of mint tea. Some recipes use only the mint, but others are based on ordinary tea flavoured with mint. The recipe for ginger mint tea, here, is a more elaborate version of iced tea using ginger mint and a touch of fresh ginger. It can also be used as a base for a more potent drink: just add rum, whisky or bourbon with some soda or mineral water to make it sparkling.

Mint is not only used in cold, sweet recipes, but also in many savoury dishes. The herb has always been considered an aid to the digestion of rich foods. In Britain, there is a long tradition of serving mint sauce as a condiment for spring lamb. The sauce is thought to have been introduced into Britain by the Romans. Another British tradition is to flavour the first new potatoes or peas of the year with mint; just add sprigs of mint to the boiling water. Though mint is not often used in French cooking, it does appear frequently in cuisines from North Africa, Spain, Italy, India and the Middle East.

Another dish which benefits from the addition of chopped mint is salad. Use fresh, chopped mint instead of chives or parsley in mixed lettuce or potato salads. Mint can be used in a tomato salad when basil is scarce. Mint is a particularly good herb to use with rice, dried beans, and bulghur wheat. A salad of green or continental lentils, generously dressed with chopped mint, makes a superb summer dish. The Arab bread salad, *fattoush*, includes mint as one of the ingredients, and it is an excellent dish to try.

Ginger mint tea

SERVES 4

2 teaspoons China tea
2½ pints (1.4 litres) water
A piece of fresh ginger root, about 1 inch (2.5 cm)
  long, roughly chopped
A handful of fresh ginger mint (or substitute
  ordinary garden mint), roughly chopped
Ice-cubes
Sugar, to taste
Strawberries or other summer fruit, sliced

Put the China tea in a heatproof jug. Boil ½ pint (300 ml) of the water and pour over the leaves. Add the mint, the fresh ginger root, and a little sugar to taste. You may prefer to leave it unsweetened. Leave the mixture to infuse for about 15 minutes, then strain the liquid and pour it into a glass jug. Fill with the rest of the water and add plenty of ice. Float sprigs of mint and a few slices of strawberries on the surface.

THIS MIDDLE EASTERN COMBINATION OF FLAVOURS IS DELICIOUS. THE EARTHY TASTE OF BROWN LENTILS IS OFFSET BY THE CLEAN FLAVOUR OF MINT.

MINT TEAS, BOTH HOT AND ICED, ARE REFRESHING DRINKS. IN THIS VERSION, GINGER ROOT ADDS A SPICY TASTE AND REINFORCES THE FLAVOUR OF GINGER MINT.

Lentil & mint salad

SERVES 4–6

7 oz (200 g) dried green lentils, washed and drained
1¼ pint (750 ml) water
½ red onion or 3 spring onions, whole
A handful of fresh mint leaves
Salad dressing (see right)
½ red onion or 3 spring onions, finely chopped
Chopped mint, for garnishing

Put the lentils in a large saucepan with the water and half the whole onion, or 3 spring onions. Add in a few whole stems of mint. Bring to the boil, then reduce heat and simmer very slowly until the lentils are cooked, which may take up to 1 hour. The lentils should be soft, but still whole. Do not allow them to get mushy.

When the lentils are cooked, drain them and remove the mint and onion. While still hot, pour over the dressing. Add the chopped onion, and mix thoroughly. Finely chop or snip the remaining mint leaves and add to the mixture. Mix again and leave to cool for 1–2 hours for the flavours to develop. Garnish with chopped mint, and serve with pita bread and a leafy salad.

SALAD DRESSING

6 tablespoons olive oil
2 tablespoons wine vinegar
1 garlic clove, crushed
Salt and pepper

Make the dressing by combining the vinegar and garlic, then adding in the olive oil, bit by bit, mixing constantly.

Bergamot

MONARDA DIDYMA

Early settlers in North America discovered bergamot growing wild. It is a native of damp, slightly acid woodlands in the north-eastern United States and in Canada. The Oswego Indians used it for a tea leaf, and the plant is often known as Oswego tea. Other common names are bee balm, sweet bergamot and mountain balm. Bergamot tea first became widely drunk after the Boston Tea Party in America, when the British imports were boycotted.

Bergamot is an attractive plant with tall stems and light green, ovate leaves. The leaves are rather coarse and look somewhat like mint leaves. In fact, the plant is vaguely related to mint. The whorled flower heads are vivid red, purplish pink or, sometimes, pale pink in colour. The herb is often found growing in gardens as a decorative herbaceous border plant, but the fragrant, orange-scented quality of the flowers and leaves place the plant in the herb classification.

The scent of the plant is reminiscent of true bergamot, which is *Citrus bergamia*, a citrus tree, and a completely different plant. Oil of bergamot is made from the rind of the fruit of this tree, and the herb bergamot is so named because its fragrance is like that of the tree's fruit. The scent of both plants is a warm, minty orange. The famous Earl Grey tea is a blend of China tea flavoured with oil of bergamot.

Bergamot is a perennial which grows best in moist, rich soils. It does have the habit of slowly dying off from the centre, so, ideally, plants should be lifted, divided, and replanted every few years to keep them healthy and vigorous.

Fresh bergamot leaves have many purposes, though they are chiefly used for making herb tea. The tea is thought to have relaxing properties, so it is a good night-time drink. The leaves are particularly suitable for using in salads; scatter some chopped leaves over a beetroot salad and use a dressing made with orange juice and a little grated orange peel to accentuate the bergamot flavour. Bergamot also works well with pork dishes; spread chopped leaves on pork before roasting or grilling, or else include the chopped leaves in a stuffing for rich meats. Some recipes include bergamot flowers in infusions. Many kinds of summer drinks and salads look spectacular decorated with the bold flowers, though check for insects hiding in the long corollas. If necessary, float the flowers in water to dislodge lurking earwigs.

The leaves can be dried and used in the same way as the fresh leaves, but they do tend to lose their flavour. The plant is dormant during the winter, so some dried leaves are convenient to have in store during this season.

THE PURPLE FLOWERS OF BERGAMOT LOOK ENCHANTING PLANTED NEXT TO SUNNY MARIGOLDS IN A GARDEN.

BERGAMOT TEA HAS BEEN DRUNK FOR CENTURIES WHEN INDIAN AND CHINA TEAS HAVE BEEN UNAVAILABLE. MAKE IT FOR A SPECIAL TEA-TIME, USING YOUR BEST CHINA.

Oswego tea

— • —

SERVES 3—4

3 tablespoons chopped, fresh bergamot leaves
1½ pints (900 ml) boiling water
Honey or sugar, to taste

Put the leaves in a teapot and pour on the boiling water. Stir well and leave to infuse in a warm place for up to 10 minutes. Strain the tea into cups and serve with honey or sugar to sweeten, but without milk.

For guests or for a special treat, you may like to serve the hot drink in a teapot, along with a plate of crisp almond biscuits.

Sweet Cicely

MYRRHIS ODORATA

In northern Europe and North America, sweet cicely grows wild along roadsides and in woodlands. In early summer, it blooms with a profusion of creamy white flowers above lush foliage.

Sweet cicely is a handsome plant, suitable for any flower border or herb garden. It is a perennial and easy to grow, eventually reaching about 2–5 feet (60–150 cm) in height. It can be grown from seed in the spring in position, or else seed can be sown into small pots and then the seedlings transplanted later. If allowed to flower and seed, mature plants will produce many small seedlings round the original plant; these can also be transplanted out to new positions. Sweet cicely prefers good soil, which does not dry out, and partial shade.

In the past, many parts of the plant were used. The seeds were once pounded into a paste to polish furniture, and steeped in brandy to be taken as a cure for indigestion. The roots were boiled or grated and eaten raw in salads; they were thought to be especially nourishing for elderly people. There were also recipes for candying the roots to make a mock stem ginger. The leaves reduce the need for sweeteners in dishes; for centuries, they have been cooked with tart fruits, such as rhubarb and gooseberries, to save on the quantity of sugar needed.

In addition to the sweetness of the leaves, there is also a slight aniseed taste, rather like the taste of chervil. This flavour combines well with sour fruits. The appearance of the fresh young leaves happily coincides with the first harvests of early summer garden fruit, making the leaf and fruit perfect partners for summer recipes. Add a spoonful of chopped sweet cicely leaves in poached rhubarb, gooseberries or apricots, and use slightly less sugar than usual.

THIS VARIATION ON AN OLD RECIPE IS WELL WORTH TRYING. THE SWEET CICELY GENTLY FLAVOURS AND SWEETENS THE APPLE FILLING OF THE TART.

Apple & sweet cicely tart

•

SERVES 6—8

SHORTCRUST PASTRY

6 oz (175 g) unsalted butter
8 oz (225 g) plain flour
1½ oz (40 g) caster sugar
1 egg yolk
Cold water

TART FILLING

1½ lbs (700 g) cooking apples
2 oz (50 g) butter
3 oz (75 g) sugar
Grated peel and juice of 1 lemon
A handful of sweet cicely leaves, finely chopped
Icing sugar, to decorate

To make the pastry, rub the butter into the flour and add sugar. Then stir in egg yolk and mix with enough water to make a firm dough. Leave to stand for 30 minutes.

Meanwhile, peel, core and slice the apples. Then make the tart filling by cooking the apples in a heavy saucepan with the butter and sugar for about 10 minutes, until tender. Remove the apple mixture from the heat, and add lemon peel and juice. Leave to cool.

Roll out the pastry dough and line a 10-inch (25-cm) springform tart tin, either trimming the pastry to the edge or leaving ragged. Reserve the remaining dough to make a lattice top for the tart. Bake blind in the oven at 200°C (400°F) Mark 6 for 15 minutes, then remove.

Add sweet cicely to the cooled apple mixture and pour into the tart case. Using the remaining dough, make lattice strips by rolling out pastry and cutting ½ inch-(1 cm-) wide strips. Weave the strips over the top of the tart. Return to the oven and bake for an additional 15 minutes until the pastry is golden and the filling is bubbling. Sprinkle the icing sugar thickly on the top and serve the tart warm.

Basil

OCIMUM BASILICUM

Basil is a soft-leaved, pungent annual beloved in Mediterranean countries, where it grows well. It is found wild in tropical and sub-tropical areas of the world, and is widely cultivated for its culinary usefulness. In colder climates, basil succeeds outdoors in good summers if given a rich, free-draining soil and plenty of sun. However, it is often better grown in pots or under glass for the best crop. The seeds may be sown in a greenhouse and set out into the ground in spring, after the frost has finished. For an abundant and long-lasting display, sow another crop of seeds during the summer. Two-lipped flowers are also produced, and these vary in colour from white to red; some have a purplish tint. The flowering shoots should be pinched out as early as possible to promote the growth of more leaves.

The various forms of basil include a bush type with many small leaves on a low, bushy plant, as well as sweet basil, which makes a taller, upright plant with larger leaves. Also available are a decorative purple-leaved variety and Italian basil, which has exceptionally large leaves.

Basil is first and foremost a culinary herb, though it was also used in the past as a medicinal plant. In Caribbean folklore, basil is associated with love and prosperity; sprinkling basil water over a shop or business is thought to attract buyers and profits. Its warm, sweet, spicy scent is certainly alluring and powerful, and is similar to cloves. It is a versatile herb with a warm, balsamy flavour that perfectly complements tomatoes, eggs and cheese. Basil is also useful in salads, meat or chicken dishes, and with fish. It is the main ingredient of the classic Italian pesto sauce, which is traditionally served with pasta and soup dishes. Basil is best used fresh and is thought to aid in digestion as well as stimulate the appetite. The delicious flavour of basil is very powerful, so use this herb with care.

Freezing basil

Basil can be dried, but a much better result is produced if it is frozen. Simply place whole leaves or stems in small plastic bags and seal tightly. Label the bags and freeze. When the herb is required, simply break a little off the frozen mixture and crumble it straight into the dish. It is also easier to chop when frozen, but should only be used for flavouring and not for garnishing, as thawed leaves lose their crispness. The best way to use frozen basil is in dishes, such as casseroles or stews, where the appearance of the herb is not important. Do not refreeze frozen basil once it has thawed.

FROZEN BASIL IS USEFUL IN THE AUTUMN AND WINTER, WHEN THE FRESH LEAVES ARE NOT AVAILABLE.

THE CLASSIC ITALIAN PESTO SAUCE IS A WONDERFULLY DISTINCTIVE PARTNER TO PASTA AND OTHER SAVOURY DISHES.

Summer vegetable soup with pesto

•

SERVES 4

This delicious soup is perfect for high summer, when fresh basil and vegetables are plentiful.

4 oz (120 g) dried cannellini beans
1 small onion, chopped
Olive oil
2 garlic cloves, crushed
3 ripe tomatoes, skinned
8 oz (225 g) fine French beans, chopped
3 small courgettes, sliced
3 pints (2 litres) water
1 oz (30 g) shell-shaped pasta
Salt and pepper, to taste
Grated Parmesan cheese

Soak the beans overnight, then boil in fresh water for 10 minutes, then simmer for about 30 minutes until soft. Reserve the cooking water. Soften the onion in a little olive oil in a saucepan and add the garlic. After 3 minutes, add the tomatoes and stew a little longer. Add the French beans and the courgettes. Cook for 5 minutes over a medium heat, then add the water, cannellini beans and their cooking liquid, pasta, and salt and pepper to taste. Cook for a further 15 minutes. Serve in soup bowls with a spoonful of pesto sauce and a sprinkling of grated Parmesan cheese in each bowl.

PESTO SAUCE

¾ pint (500 ml) fresh basil leaves, torn
2 oz (60 g) pine kernels
1 garlic clove, crushed
2 oz (60 g) grated Parmesan cheese
About 6 fl oz (180 ml) olive oil

Using a pestle and mortar, pound together the basil leaves, pine kernels, garlic and half the cheese. When the mixture takes on a creamy consistency, gradually add the oil and the rest of the cheese. The sauce should be soft and smooth in texture.

As basil is the perfect accompaniment to tomatoes, plant basil between rows of tomato plants to serve as a reminder to use the fruit and herb together. There is a theory that the two plants are good companions, keeping each other free of pests and diseases. Any tomato-based dish benefits from the addition of basil, including lasagne and spaghetti sauces, such as bolognese or neapolitan. The easiest and quickest way to enjoy basil and tomato is in a simple salad. Large, ripe tomatoes, sliced and sprinkled with olive oil, lemon juice, and a handful of basil leaves, are one of the delights of summer.

The flavour of basil is at its best when eaten raw; even in hot dishes, it is scattered on at the last minute or cooked very briefly to preserve the flavour. Fresh basil is delicious in all sorts of pasta dishes, with or without tomatoes, and a sprinkling of snipped basil leaves adds a touch of green to the patriotic colour scheme of Italian cheese crostini.

Crostini are little rounds of toasted bread which should be served before a meal as an hors-d'oeuvre or alongside a starter. Traditionally, they have many kinds of toppings; sometimes the topping is made from a liver pâté and at other times a tomato and anchovy mixture. Ripe and succulent tomatoes used alone with just a touch of garlic is another choice, but the melted mixture of mozzarella cheese with tomato and basil, in the recipe on the right, is simply delectable.

Fresh tomato & basil salad

Choose well-flavoured, fresh tomatoes which are fleshy and without too much juice. Just prior to serving, slice them and spread the slices in a single layer on a flat serving dish. Sprinkle on a vinaigrette made from olive oil, lemon juice, and salt and pepper to taste. Then add whole, fresh basil leaves on top. For a more substantial dish, include layers of mozzarella cheese.

THE ENTICING SMELL OF CROSTINI, SPRINKLED WITH FRESH BASIL WHILE STILL HOT, IS MOUTH-WATERING.

A SIMPLE TOMATO AND BASIL SALAD IS THE PERFECT DISH TO EAT OUTDOORS, ESPECIALLY WITH PICNIC FOOD OR BARBECUED MEAT.

Basil crostini

•

SERVES 4

1 small, narrow French loaf
Butter, softened, for spreading
4 oz (100 g) mozzarella cheese
1 very ripe tomato, skinned and seeded (substitute
  tinned tomatoes if yours are not ripe enough)
6 anchovy fillets, washed to remove excess salt
6 large, fresh basil leaves

Cut the bread into thin rings and butter
sparingly on both sides. Lay the rings on a
buttered baking tray. Slice the mozzarella cheese
thinly, and lay a piece on each bread ring. Slice

the tomato flesh into small strips and halve each
anchovy fillet. Lay a strip of tomato and
anchovy criss-cross on each ring.

Bake in a hot oven at 200°C (400°F) Mark 6
for 12–15 minutes. Keep a careful watch on the
crostini and do not let them over-cook. The
bread should be toasted and the cheese just
melted; if the mozzarella is over-cooked, it
hardens and becomes stringy. When removing
the crostini from the oven, snip a scattering of
fresh basil over each one. Serve while very hot,
accompanied by red Italian country wine.

PLASTIC CARTONS
OF FRESH HERBS
ARE A WELCOME
NEW DEVELOPMENT
FOR THE COOK.
THEY WILL LAST
FOR SEVERAL DAYS
IF YOU HARVEST
THEM JUDICIOUSLY.

Basil is one herb which happily grows in a container indoors. For many people, this is the easiest way to cultivate it successfully. It demands warmth and sunshine but also plenty of moisture at its roots. Even in good summers in temperate regions it usually prefers the protection of a glasshouse, but it can be grown on a sunny window-sill.

Basil germinates readily from seed and the little seedlings can be transplanted to a suitable pot containing any good, fertile soil or compost. The plants will grow quickly; picking the centre of the growing plant regularly will inhibit flowering and the plant will then produce maximum leaf. Once the plant has flowered, leaf production is poor and the whole plant deteriorates.

Many food stores now sell small plastic cartons of growing herbs, and basil is a good choice to buy. Though designed to last just a short time, but to offer really fresh herbs during that time, these little containers will, in fact, last two or three weeks with just the odd watering to keep them fresh. Stand them in a light, warm place.

One of the best ways of capturing the summery flavour of basil is to steep the fresh leaves in wine vinegar or oil. Bottles of flavoured oils and vinegars are a welcome sight in the storecupboard through the winter months.

Basil oil

— • —

Choose strongly scented, fresh basil leaves which you have grown, or else buy a bunch of leaves or a growing plant. If you pick your own leaves, do so during the middle of the morning, before the sun is very hot but when the plant's volatile oils are at their peak. Avoid washing the leaves unless they are dirty or you do not know their origins. If you do wash the leaves, dry them gently by patting them with a clean cloth; the soft leaves are easily damaged.

Use clean and dry jars or bottles with sealable stoppers. Put leaves or whole stems of basil into the jars. One or two stems are enough, but you can be as generous as you please. Pour a light, well-flavoured olive oil over the leaves, or use sunflower or safflower oil if you prefer. Close the tops of the bottles securely, and leave them to stand in a sunny window-sill for a few days. Then move the bottles to a cool storecupboard and leave for several weeks. After this period, you may like to remove the basil leaves, which will have lost their freshness. If the bottle is for a gift, a new sprig or leaf can be added just before giving it away. Use the oil in dressings and for pizzas and tomato dishes.

OLIVE OIL SOAKS UP
THE WARM,
AROMATIC FLAVOUR
OF FRESH BASIL.
STORE BASIL OIL TO
USE IN SALADS AND
SAUCES AFTER THE
SUMMER SEASON
IS OVER.

Marjoram

ORIGANUM

There are three main species of marjoram in the *Origanum* genus that are grown for their scent and culinary use. Sweet marjoram, also called knotted or garden marjoram, is botanically *Origanum marjorana,* and native to Europe; it is frequently used in French cuisine. Oregano, *Origanum vulgare,* is also called wild or common marjoram and is also native to Europe, but most often used in Italian dishes. Pot marjoram, *Origanum onites,* is native to the Mediterranean and used extensively in Greek cuisine.

Differences in the common names are regional; in Italy, oregano is known as *origano,* and in Greece all marjorams are known as *rigani.* Even within the same species of marjoram, variations in taste are evident, depending on the area where the plant is grown. The word marjoram derives from two words in Greek, meaning 'the joy of the mountain'. All marjorams have a sweet, warm taste and all prefer well-drained soil and a sunny position.

Sweet marjoram is the most useful species to grow. It makes a compact plant with reddish stems, grey leaves and insignificant white flowers which are arranged in knots, hence one of its common names. Even though it is a perennial, it is best treated as an annual or half-hardy annual and sown in spring to be planted out in early summer. Sowings in late summer or early autumn can be potted up and brought indoors to provide leaves throughout winter.

Oregano is found growing on calcareous soils, and the plant has attractive, downy, purplish stems with deep purple-pink flowers in late summer. The variety 'Aureum' has golden yellow foliage, which makes it highly decorative for a garden. Oregano has a stronger taste and scent than the delicate-tasting sweet marjoram.

Marjoram has always been known as 'a herb of happiness', and it has many pleasant associations. It was once wound into garlands to be worn by brides and bridegrooms to bring them a happy life ahead, and eating marjoram was considered to have a 'nourishing effect' on the brain. At one time, its uses were both medicinal and culinary; herbal tobaccos and snuffs were made from the powdered leaves, marjoram oil was added to hair tonics, and fresh marjoram leaves were strewn on floors as 'strewing herbs'. Lotions made from marjoram were used to relieve the swelling of painful joints affected by rheumatism, and tisanes were taken as a preventative for seasickness. Marjoram was included in remedies for bronchitis, colds and sore throats. The dried leaves, particularly from sweet marjoram, were a popular ingredient for sweet bags and pot-pourris, as the flavour and aroma are not spoiled in the drying process, unlike many other herbs.

OREGANO HAS ROUND, GREEN LEAVES AND DENSE GROWTH. THE FLOWERS APPEAR IN LATE SUMMER AND ARE FULL OF NECTAR, WHICH ATTRACTS INSECTS, INCLUDING BUTTERFLIES, TO THE HERB GARDEN.

AMBER-COLOURED APPLE JELLY MAKES THE BASE FOR A PRESERVE FLAVOURED WITH SWEET MARJORAM. SERVE THE JELLY WITH ROASTED OR GRILLED MEAT.

Traditionally, marjoram is used with meat and game, and with robust tastes and textures. A delicious idea is to make a jelly, flavoured with marjoram, to eat with roasts and grills.

Marjoram jelly

Use a basic recipe for a sour fruit jelly, based on cooking apples or gooseberries. At the final boiling stage, when the sugar and juice are added, include whole sprigs of marjoram, preferably sweet marjoram. Remove the marjoram pieces before potting up the jelly, but replace them with a fresh sprig of the herb.

Oregano is the type of marjoram used in many familiar Mediterranean recipes. One of the best, and most delicious, summer lunch dishes is a Greek salad made from fresh, ripe tomatoes, cucumber and feta cheese. Oregano is used in a wide range of Italian dishes, such as pasta recipes, as it adds spice and aroma to tomato sauce. It is also an indispensible part of pizza.

The recipe on page 91 makes a dish that is a cross between a pizza and a *pissaladière*. The oregano flavours the pepper mixture and is used to create the lattice effect. Make this dish when you have time to make a home-made bread dough, rather than using a ready-made pizza base.

Greek salad

·

SERVES 4

This will make a superb light lunch served with fresh bread.

Lettuce or Belgium endive leaves, washed
  and shredded
6 small tomatoes, cubed
1 small cucumber, peeled and cubed
6 oz (175 g) feta cheese, cubed
4 oz (100 g) black olives
A bunch of fresh sweet marjoram or oregano
Salad dressing (see right)

Line a shallow serving dish with the lettuce or
Belgium endive leaves. Put the cubed tomatoes,
cucumber and cheese on the bed of lettuce and
scatter the olives over them. Pour over the

dressing and scatter the marjoram leaves
throughout, mixing lightly.

SALAD DRESSING

1 tablespoon lemon juice
Salt and pepper
3 tablespoons olive oil

Combine the lemon juice and salt and pepper,
then add the olive oil, bit by bit, mixing
constantly. Alternatively, shake all the
ingredients in a screw-top jar.

Tomato, red pepper & oregano pizza

•

MAKES 1 LARGE PIZZA, FOR 3—4

PIZZA DOUGH

Large pinch of salt
1 packet easy-blend dried yeast
7 oz (200 g) plain white flour
1 tablespoon olive oil
About 1 cup warm water
Olive oil, for brushing

PIZZA TOPPING

2 tablespoons olive oil
2 onions, finely chopped
3 garlic cloves, crushed
1 lb (450 g) ripe plum tomatoes
1 tablespoon tomato purée
2 red peppers
Salt and pepper
2 tablespoons chopped, fresh oregano
Pinch of sugar
Black olives and oregano leaves,
*   to garnish*

To make the dough, add the dried yeast and salt to the flour. Then add the oil and mix by hand or in a food processor, adding enough warm water to make a soft dough. Cover and leave to rise in a warm place for 2 hours.

To make the topping, heat the oil in a saucepan, and add the onions and garlic. Cook until softened, but not brown, then add tomatoes, tomato purée and 1 red pepper, chopped into small strips. Season with salt and pepper, then add the chopped oregano and the pinch of sugar. Leave to cook over a low heat, uncovered, for about 20 minutes, until the topping is thick and most of the liquid has evaporated.

Meanwhile, char the remaining red pepper under a hot grill. Then put it inside a plastic bag for 5 minutes to steam, which makes it easier to peel. Remove the blackened skin and cut the flesh into long, narrow strips.

When the dough has risen, knock it down and roll out to a large circle, keeping the edge thicker the whole way round. Put it on a large, flat baking tray and spread the topping over it. Make a lattice pattern with the strips of red pepper. Make alternate rows of black olives and oregano leaves in the diamond spaces. Brush all over with olive oil and bake at 230°C (450°F) Mark 8 for about 15–20 minutes.

FETA CHEESE, TOMATOES, OLIVES, CUCUMBER, FRUITY OLIVE OIL AND PLENTY OF FRESH MARJORAM LEAVES ADD A GREEK TASTE TO A LUNCH-TIME SALAD.

GOOD PIZZA REQUIRES THE FLAVOUR OF OREGANO IN THE TOMATO MIXTURE. HERE, OREGANO LEAVES STUD THE SURFACE BESIDE GLOSSY OLIVES.

Poppy

PAPAVER

The poppy family produces some of the most beautiful and colourful flowers in the plant world. There are both perennial and annual species, and the one used for its seed is *Papaver somniferum*, the opium poppy. The plant most often grown in the garden is the field poppy, or corn poppy, known botanically as *Papaver rhoeas*.

The opium poppy has flowers in shades of pink, red and mauve, and in both single and double forms, and grows taller than the field poppy. It is a flower of great age, probably originating in the Middle East, but certainly grown around the Mediterranean from medieval times. By the sixteenth century, the seeds were being recommended for their flavouring and decorative properties, but they had probably been used in these ways for centuries. The opiate is collected from the juice of the capsule which surrounds the seed, but the opiate is not contained in the seed itself. At one time, poppy seed heads were used to make a crude medicine to soothe muscle strain, sprains and neuralgia; a lotion was applied with hot flannels.

Annual poppies prefer ordinary, well-drained soil in the sun. They can be sown from seed in early spring, and then thinned out. Remove the dead flowers of the opium poppy if you do not want seed. Opium poppy flowers have a brief life of only a few days. Once the petals fall, and if the flower has been fertilized, the seed capsule swells and ripens, holding hundreds of tiny greyish seeds. When the capsule is fully ripe and dry, small holes open at the top and the seed is scattered, as if from a pepper-pot. There is also a variety of opium poppy which produces cream-coloured seeds.

The dried seed heads, either full or empty of seeds, make dramatic flower arrangements. If they can be harvested and dried to preserve their special green-blue colour, so much the better, but they look just as attractive when bronze-brown. Mix them with other dried flowers or herbs, or use them alone to display their shape and texture to best advantage. For beautiful Christmas decorations, try lightly gilding the seed heads with a spray paint.

In many parts of Europe, there is a long tradition for using the delicious, nutty-tasting seeds lavishly in sweet cakes and breads. The seeds are often scattered over egg-brushed bread doughs before baking to create a pretty decoration and crunchy crust. There are also recipes for enriched bread doughs with sweet fillings of crushed poppy seeds, such as the Polish bread, *strucla*.

THE DRIED SEED HEADS OF THE OPIUM POPPY ARE EXQUISITELY DETAILED. THE BLUE-GREEN BLOOM IS BEAUTIFUL, AND THE TOP EDGE LOOKS GILDED.

THE NUTTY CRUNCHINESS OF DRIED POPPY SEEDS HAS LONG BEEN APPRECIATED IN EUROPEAN CUISINE. THIS POPPY SEED RING LOOKS ELABORATE, BUT IS NOT DIFFICULT TO MAKE.

Poppy seed ring

•

MAKES 1

This recipe is based on Polish strucla. You will need to make the filling the night before.

POPPY SEED FILLING

5 oz (150 g) poppy seeds
Boiling water
3 oz (75 g) granulated sugar
1 oz (25 g) blanched almonds, chopped
1 oz (25 g) currants
1 tablespoon brandy
1 dessert spoon clear honey
Juice of ½ lemon
Few drops almond essence
1 egg white

BREAD DOUGH

½ oz (15 g) dried yeast
1 tablespoon warm water
8 oz (225 g) strong white flour
2 fl oz (50 ml) warm milk
2 egg yolks
1 egg white
3 oz (75 g) granulated sugar
Grated peel of 1 orange
Grated peel of 1 lemon
Pinch of salt
½ teaspoon vanilla essence
1 oz (25 g) butter
egg yolk and water mix, to brush

To make the filling, put poppy seeds in a bowl and cover with boiling water. Let stand 1 hour. Drain, then grind the seeds in a pestle and mortar. Mix in the sugar, almonds, currants, brandy, honey, lemon juice, and almond essence. Stir in the egg white to obtain a moist consistency. Chill overnight.

To make the dough, dissolve the yeast in the warm water. Add half the flour and the warm milk, mixing well. Leave in a warm place.

Beat together the egg yolks, egg white, sugar, grated citrus peels, salt and vanilla. Add to the first dough mixture and mix in half of the remaining flour, stirring vigorously. Melt the butter, cool it and stir in. Knead the dough by hand, or with a dough hook in an electric mixer, adding the remaining flour. Cover the dough and leave in a warm place to rise.

When the dough is double in size, knock it down and roll out to a large rectangle. Spread the filling over the dough and, starting at a long end, roll up the dough into a sausage shape. Form into a ring and pinch the ends together. Place on a baking sheet and let rise again. When double in size, brush top with the egg yolk and water mixture and snip slits into the surface. Bake at 190°C (375°F) Mark 5 for about 20 minutes, until golden and cooked throughout.

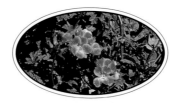

Scented Geranium

PELARGONIUM

Many people are acquainted with the dazzling flowers of geraniums, or pelargoniums, as they are correctly named. In mild climates, they are used as pot plants to decorate steps and balconies, and, in cooler regions, they have become a popular conservatory plant. Related to the showy pelargoniums are the scented-leaved types, which have highly fragrant and, often, decorative leaves. Though most scented types have smaller leaves and flowers than the larger pot and bedding geraniums, the shape and structure of the plant is, overall, very similar. Most scented geraniums make small, compact plants, which can be kept neat by a little regular trimming. They are best propagated from stem cuttings, prefer well-drained soil, and can be grown in pots.

The scents contained in these plants range from citrus to rose, and from balsam to ginger, and the plants make a fascinating and varied collection. The lemon-scented geranium, *Pelargonium crispum*, has tiny, green, frilled leaves. There is also a variety with cream-coloured edgings to the leaves. Peppermint geranium, *P. tomentosum*, has large, soft, hairy leaves with the scent of peppermint. *Pelargonium* x *fragrans* has silvery grey leaves, which smell of pine, and *P. quercifolium* is almond-scented. Rose-scented geranium, *P. graveolens*, has the fragrance of 'attar of roses', and the dried leaves are useful for pot-pourris. The apple-scented geranium is *P. odoratissimum*, and a coconut-scented type is *P. enossulariodes*. Other types of scented geraniums are 'Clorinda', which smells of eucalyptus; 'Endsleigh', which is pepper-scented; and 'Prince of Orange', which has an orange scent.

Many of the scented types originate from South Africa, and the plants first reached northern Europe in the seventeenth century. Two hundred years later, they were seen in the glasshouses of the wealthy as well as on the window-sills of the poor; they were universally loved for their cheerful habit, constantly green leaves, and delicious scents. In Britain, the Victorians were particularly fond of the plants; they would place them in pots along paths and on terraces in the summer, and bring them indoors in winter.

Any of the most pleasantly scented geraniums can be used for cooking. The leaves should be used fresh, as they will lose flavour if dried. Traditionally, the leaves were used to flavour sugar, to scent milk-based puddings and custards, and to flavour jellies and preserves. During the period when finger bowls were common sights on dining tables, a leaf of lemon-scented geranium was always floated in the bowls. A leaf was often picked on the way to church and kept in a pocket or prayer book and pressed to release the fragrance.

Lemon geranium mousse

·

SERVES 4—6

This light, lemony mousse is flavoured with lemon-scented geranium, but you may like to substitute an orange-scented geranium.

5 fl oz (150 ml) double cream
Finely grated peel and juice of 1 lemon
6 fresh lemon-scented geranium leaves
6 oz (175 g) caster sugar
4 large eggs, separated
½ oz (15 g) gelatine
5 fl oz (15 ml) water
Scented geranium leaves and flowers, to decorate

Heat the cream gently with the lemon peel and geranium leaves. Leave to cool.

Beat the sugar and egg yolks until thick, then add in the lemon juice.

Sprinkle the gelatine on the water. Place the gelatine in a small saucepan over a low heat until it has dissolved completely. Pouring from a height, fold the gelatine into the egg-yolk mixture. Whisk constantly, then put to one side until it begins to thicken.

Strain the cooled cream to remove the peel and leaves, and whisk until slightly thickened. Then fold it into the mousse mixture. Stiffly beat the egg whites and fold into the mousse. Pour into individual dessert dishes and chill thoroughly until set. Decorate with fresh geranium leaves and flowers before serving.

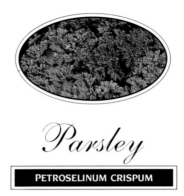

Parsley

PETROSELINUM CRISPUM

Parsley, with its mild taste and pretty, fresh, green leaves, is one of the most commonly used kitchen herbs. In the past, parsley was an ingredient for medicines and herbal cures, but today it appears throughout the year as a useful garnish and flavour in all manner of savoury foods. A member of the umbellifer family, parsley is a hardy biennial, but it is often grown as an annual to keep the kitchen in fresh supplies. If grown as a biennial, parsley will flower and set seed in the second year, and then the leaf quality deteriorates before the whole plant dies down.

The parsley plant has branching stems and greenish yellow summer flowers, and there are two types: curled-leaf and flat-leaf. Curled-leaf parsley, *P. crispum crispum*, is the most decorative,

and makes a small, round hummock of bright green. This type was developed to be used as a garnish. Flat-leaved parsley, *P. crispum tuberosum*, is also called French parsley. It is a more straggly plant with weaker stems, but it is claimed to have better flavour. A keen cook is likely to want both sorts of parsley in quantity.

Parsley is normally grown from seed, but it is very slow to germinate and can sometimes take three or four weeks to appear. Soaking the seeds overnight before planting, or watering with hot water after seeds are planted, can speed up germination. It is often best to sow seed into trays or pots, and then to transplant the seedlings when they appear. Grow parsley in good soil and keep it well watered. Protect the herb from hard frost and severe weather with a cloche during winter; this will maintain parsley and provide a crop right through the year. If it is easier, pot a plant and keep it in a greenhouse.

Curled-leaf parsley makes a pretty, low edging to paths. It also looks attractive when planted at the front of a herb garden. It is one herb which should, ideally, be grown near the kitchen, though a bunch of parsley kept in water will stay fresh for several days.

Parsley is high in vitamins A and C. It is often used in conjunction with other herbs, such as in *fines herbes* (see page 22) or in bouquet garnis (see page 55). The flavour is most concentrated in the stems, which can be added whole to stocks and soups and removed before eating. It is rarely used as the main ingredient in a recipe, except in salsas, or chutneys. The salsa recipe, on the right, is quick and easy to make, and is perfect for accompanying plain foods, such as cold chicken, cold roast meat or *charcuterie*.

A POT OF CURLED-LEAF PARSLEY IS HANDY FOR THE KITCHEN, BUT THE HERB ALSO MAKES AN ATTRACTIVE EDGING IN A GARDEN.

Salsa verde

—— • ——

SERVES 6—8

You may prefer to omit the anchovies in this recipe, or adjust the seasonings to acquire a balance that suits your taste. Serve with a selection of charcuterie, such as parma ham and proscuitto.

IN A MATTER OF
SECONDS, YOU CAN
CREATE THIS
FABULOUS GREEN
SAUCE FROM
PARSLEY,
ANCHOVIES, OIL
AND BREADCRUMBS.

2 oz (50 g) fresh parsley, chopped
1 tablespoon snipped chives or spring onion tops
½ tablespoon chopped fresh basil or mint
½ oz (15 g) fresh breadcrumbs
4 anchovy fillets, drained if tinned, and finely chopped
1 garlic clove, crushed
4 fl oz (100 ml) olive oil
2 tablespoons lemon juice
Salt and pepper

Put the herbs, breadcrumbs, anchovies and garlic into a food processor or liquidizer. Add 1 tablespoon from the oil and 1 tablespoon from the lemon juice. Process to a paste, then gradually add in the remaining oil and lemon juice while processing.

Taste and adjust seasoning by adding salt and pepper, if necessary. Once made, the salsa will keep for several days in the refrigerator if covered tightly.

Spaghetti with parsley & garlic sauce

•

SERVES 4 AS A MAIN COURSE

Use the best ingredients you can find: good pasta, virgin olive oil and fresh parsley.
Serve with Italian bread and plenty of red wine.

1 lb (450 g) spaghetti
6 tablespoons olive oil
2 garlic cloves, crushed
4 tablespoons chopped, fresh parsley
Salt and pepper

Bring a large saucepan of salted water to the boil and begin to cook the spaghetti. Heat the oil in a smaller saucepan, and add the garlic, cooking very gently over a low heat. Do not allow the garlic to brown. When the pasta is ready, drain it well and return it to the pan. Pour over the oil and garlic, then add in the parsley and season with salt and pepper. Mix quickly and thoroughly. Serve the spaghetti immediately on warmed plates.

In legend, the ancient Romans used parsley to counteract drunkenness, and in Greece it was a symbol of death. It was used as a grave decoration, but garlands of parsley were also awarded at games. However, these games owed their tradition to games played at funerals, so even in this case, the herb was linked to death. By the Middle Ages, parsley was associated with death and the devil, and transplanting the herb in the garden was thought to bring tragedy to the home.

Curled-leaf parsley was popular in Victorian times, and was used to garnish all kinds of savoury dishes, from plates of sandwiches to poached salmon. Deep-fried parsley sprigs were a favourite to accompany fish in the 1930s; the normally soft leaves turn crisp and brittle in hot oil.

Parsley can be used in generous quantities in soups, sauces and stuffings, or as a garnish for shellfish, fish, meat, poultry, game and vegetable dishes. There are few British recipes which use parsley on its own, but parsley is used in great quantities in the Middle East, particularly in the well-known bulghur wheat salad, tabbouleh.

Tabbouleh

— • —

SERVES 6

4 oz (100 g) bulghur wheat
2 tablespoons lemon juice
4 tablespoons olive oil
Salt and pepper
2 oz (50 g) fresh parsley, finely chopped
4 spring onions, finely chopped
2 tablespoons finely chopped, fresh mint
3 tomatoes, skinned and diced
½ cucumber, peeled, salted and drained for ½ hour, then rinsed and chopped

Put the wheat in a large shallow bowl. Pour boiling water over to just cover and leave for 30 minutes. If any water remains, drain well.

Put the lemon juice in a bowl and add the oil, bit by bit, stirring constantly. Season and mix into the wheat. Then add parsley, onions and mint. Leave in a cool place. Just before serving, mix in the tomato and cucumber.

BULGHUR WHEAT, TOMATOES, CUCUMBER, MINT AND LEMON JUICE ARE MIXED WITH LARGE AMOUNTS OF CHOPPED PARSLEY TO MAKE THIS TABBOULEH SALAD.

Purslane

PORTULACA OLERACEA

Purslane is an annual, and is also known as pussley, pigweed or, simply, portulaca. For centuries, it has been gathered or cultivated to make useful additions to leafy, green salads. The plant has small, juicy and succulent leaves with a mild, slightly nutty flavour. The stems are crisp and also edible. In the past, purslane leaves were pickled, often with caraway seeds, for winter store-cupboards. The seventeenth-century herbalist, Nicholas Culpeper, described various medicinal uses for purslane; he claimed that it cleansed the blood, soothed burns and wounds, and the juice from the boiled seeds healed muscle strain.

Purslane seed may be bought for either a green-leaved or a gold-leaved type. The golden purslane is very decorative in salads or in the garden, but both types are half-hardy plants, which will not stand extreme cold outdoors. The best way to grow purslane is to sow seed into small pots in late spring, then transplant the small plants outdoors when the risk of frost has passed. Sowings in late summer can provide small plants through autumn; these plants will grow sturdier if given a little protection by a cold frame. Plant purslane in light, sandy soil and in sun.

Purslane is a common ingredient in food from India, where it is known as *kulfa*. It is included in the Arab salad, fattoush, and is known as *bagli* in Arabic. In Holland, purslane is often grown as a salad crop, and, in France, where it is known as *pourpier*, purslane is included in sorrel soup. However, purslane is predominantly a raw salad leaf, but if you have a large crop, you may like to steam the herb, or stir-fry the young shoots, serving them with melted butter. Add the leaves to light vegetable soups or make delicate-tasting purslane sandwiches for an afternoon tea.

Purslane tea sandwiches

MAKES 1

Multiply the following ingredients by the number of people you are serving.

2 slices fresh bread, preferably home-made
1 tablespoon soft cream cheese
Pepper
2 tablespoons chopped fresh purslane
Parsley sprigs, to garnish

Spread 1 slice of bread with the cheese. Add a grinding of black pepper. Put the purslane on the cheese and top with the second slice of bread. Cut off the bread crusts, and cut the sandwiches into small triangles. Arrange on a plate and decorate with sprigs of parsley. Serve with hot tea, cakes, biscuits and scones.

Rose

ROSA

The *Rosa* genus contains thousands of varieties, and no one type has been used specifically for medicinal and culinary use. There are wild species of rose growing all over the world, and cultivated varieties have been profusely bred from the species. The rose as a garden plant is enormously popular throughout temperate climates, though the requirements vary for each type.

Rose breeding over the past two centuries has tended to concentrate on perfecting form and colour, often at the expense of fragrance. Therefore, many of the most scented and useful varieties for the home are from the older roses, which date back to medieval times.

Some varieties of rose are useful making both toiletries and for food recipes, but the most important prerequisite is to choose a rose with plenty of scent. The best ones are the old-fashioned roses, either the original species or those known as 'old roses'. Unfortunately, many of these may have only one flowering period during the summer. However, new hybrids have been bred which are repeat-flowering and have the scent and form of the old roses.

One of the best roses for scent, and the one still grown commercially to make 'attar of roses' is *Rosa gallica* 'Officinalis', also known as the Apothecary's rose. It has vivid, deep crimson-pink, semi-double flowers and golden stamens, and it makes a twiggy, medium-sized bush with rough, green leaves. Another variety of *Rosa gallica* is 'Versicolor', also known as 'Rosa Mundi'. The flowers of this rose are streaked with white and pink. Generally, deep pink and red roses and have the best scent and keep their colour well after drying. White petals, and some pale pink petals, tend to dry brown.

If you intend to dry rose petals for pot-pourri or other projects, pick rose petals in summer when you have a good supply. Spread petals on wire racks or in shallow baskets and leave them in a warm, airy place. On a hot, sunny day, petals may take only a few hours in a sheltered place to dry completely, but do not leave them in full sun. A very low oven is sometimes the best place to dry petals if the weather is humid.

The rose scent has perfumed lotions, pot-pourris, toilet waters and bath oils for centuries. The aroma has remained a familiar and well-loved fragrance, which shows no sign of diminishing in appeal. All kinds of toiletries can be made using fresh rose petals. Home-made varieties may not be as concentrated as those made commercially, but they are easy and fun to make.

A FEW HEALTHY ROSE BUSHES IN THE GARDEN PROVIDE ALL THE PETALS YOU NEED FOR POT-POURRI AND CULINARY USE.

PALEST PINK ROSE LOTION IS MILDLY ASTRINGENT AND REFRESHES SKIN AFTER CLEANSING. POURED INTO A PRETTY BOTTLE, IT WOULD MAKE A LOVELY GIFT.

Rose lotion

—— • ——

This is a mild astringent lotion to pat on to the skin after cleansing.

2 cups deep red rose petals, fresh or dried
1 cup spring water
1 cup white wine vinegar
½ cup rosewater (available from a chemist)

Put the rose petals in a screwtop jar. Boil the water and vinegar, and pour over. Leave for several days, shaking daily. Then add the rosewater and pour into a stoppered bottle.

vitamin C. Many of the wild species roses produce abundant crops of hips each year, such as *Rosa californica*, *Rosa damascena* and *Rosa rubiginosa*.

In the past, rose hips have been used to make drinks and preserves, and to brighten winter meals when little fresh food was available. They are the main ingredient in rose hip syrup, which can be poured over sweet desserts.

Rose hips are ripe from late summer to autumn and can be frozen or preserved after picking. The sharp, irritating seeds must be removed, as it is just the red flesh round the seeds which is used. However, if you are making a wine or syrup in which the fruit will be strained out anyway, you can leave the hips whole.

One traditional recipe is for rose hip jelly. The result is sharp and fruity, and has a beautiful colour. Make small pots of the jelly in autumn, and give them as gifts at Christmas. Write labels explaining the jelly, and suggest eating it with hot or cold roast meats and game, and as a conventional spread for bread.

Rose hip jelly

MAKES ABOUT 1 ½—2 LBS
(700—900 G)

1 lb (450 g) cooking apples, quartered and unpeeled
2 lb (900 g) rose hips, roughly chopped
About 2 pints (1.1 litres) water
Juice of 1 lemon
Granulated sugar

Put the apples and rose hips in a large saucepan and pour over water to just cover. Boil gently for about 1 hour, until fruit is very soft. Pour into a jelly bag or a square of muslin and hang up to drip over a large bowl. Do not press the fruit pulp or the jelly will be cloudy. Leave overnight.

The next day, measure out the drained juice, and, for every 1 pint (600 ml) of juice, measure 1 lb (450 g) of sugar. Put the juice and the sugar into a saucepan. Heat slowly until the sugar dissolves, then boil rapidly until a set is reached, in about 10 minutes. Skim any foam from the surface, then pour into hot, sterilized and sealable jars. When cool, seal the jars.

CROPS OF ROSE HIPS APPEAR IN LATE SUMMER AND EARLY AUTUMN. PICK SOME OF THE FREE HARVEST TO USE IN PRESERVES, DRINKS OR SYRUPS.

GLOWING GARNET ROSE HIP JELLY MAKES AN UNUSUAL AND THOUGHTFUL CHRISTMAS GIFT, ESPECIALLY FOR A CITY-DWELLER.

The most popular culinary use for roses is in triple-distilled rosewater, which is available from chemists and specialist food shops. Rosewater is used in flavouring many Asian, Indian and Middle Eastern dishes. Fresh rose petals make the prettiest edible decorations for summer desserts, and can be scattered over a finished cake or the surface of a pudding. Rose petals or leaves can also be frosted with sugar to use as decorative garnishes (see page 75). Petals can be used in icecreams, sorbets, vinegars, honey, jams and preserves. In all these recipes, a small amount of rosewater can be included to strengthen the rose flavour. Use rosewater sparingly, though, as it can be overpowering and may spoil the delicate flavour from the fresh rose petals.

Many varieties of rose produce decorative rose hips, or heps, which are the capsules surrounding the seed. Rose hips can be seen in various shapes and sizes, according to the variety of rose, but are generally a lovely, bright, glossy red or orange. As a fruit, rose hips are exceptionally high in

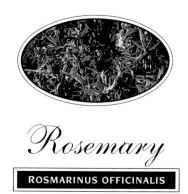

Rosemary

ROSMARINUS OFFICINALIS

———•———

Rosemary is a well-loved garden shrub and herb, grown for its grey-green, spiky leaves, pretty mauve flowers, and pungent scent. Rosemary is native to the sea cliffs of France, Italy, Spain and Greece, which is reflected in its Latin name, *Rosmarinus*, meaning 'mist of the sea'. Rosemary's tough, needle-like leaves are well-suited to salt air and buffeting by the wind, but the flowers are soft and delicate, often appearing very early in the year, or, sometimes, staying in bloom through a mild winter.

There are many varieties of rosemary from which to choose. Most have similar leaves but tend to vary in flower colour and habit of growth. The type most commonly seen makes a medium-size bush, which can grow quite wide with age; the flowers are blue-mauve in colour. There are some types which sprawl and are low-growing; these look lovely tumbling over a wall. There is a much more upright variety, 'Miss Jessup', with pale blue flowers and erect branches. 'Benenden Blue' is a lovely, deep blue-flowered variety, which is native to Corsica and Sicily. There is also the Italian 'Tuscan Blue' with equally richly coloured flowers. A variegated rosemary with splashes of yellow on the leaves was especially popular in Elizabethan times. There are varieties with white or pink flowers, which may interest collectors of unusual herbs.

Though rosemary is a herb of Mediterranean regions, it will grow successfully in more northern locations. The herb will not survive very severe winters in climates where the ground is frozen for long periods of time, or where the soil is wet and cold. Ideally, plant rosemary on a raised bed so the plant's roots will have free drainage. A huge bush of rosemary was often grown beside the door or gate of old-fashioned cottage gardens, so the rosemary leaves would release their scent when brushed against, and so a sprig could be picked and crushed when stopping at the house. A rosemary bush is excellent for even a small garden, as it is evergreen and will attract bees and other insects.

Many legends surround rosemary's history, which is not surprising considering the plant's popularity. One story associates the herb with the Virgin Mary; supposedly, she threw her blue cloak over a rosemary bush to dry, which gave the plant its pale bluish flowers. Rosemary has also become known as 'the herb of remembrance'. The ancient Greeks believed rosemary strengthened the mind and improved memory, so sprigs of the herb were twined into the hair. The herb has long been included with other flowers at funerals. In Shakespeare's *Hamlet: Act IV, Sc. v,*

THE PALE, MISTY MAUVE FLOWERS OF ROSEMARY ARE IN BLOOM FOR WEEKS ON END THROUGHOUT SPRING AND SUMMER, AND SOMETIMES RIGHT THROUGH A MILD WINTER.

Ophelia says, 'There's rosemary; that's for remembrance', serving as a plea for her to be remembered, thus foreshadowing her own death, or, possibly, emphasizing her fragile mind. Rosemary has also always been a symbol of fidelity and friendship, and a sprig was once commonly included in bride's bouquets.

Rosemary has antiseptic properties and a beautiful aroma, which makes it perfect for using as a bath herb or for hair health. The dried and crushed leaves can be used in pot-pourris or herbal sachets for the bath. Use an infusion of rosemary to add gloss and sheen to brown or black hair; rosemary also, supposedly, helps stimulate the scalp. To make an infusion, simply pour boiling water over branches of fresh or dried rosemary, leave it for several minutes, and use the infusion as a final rinse after hair-washing.

AN INFUSION OF ROSEMARY HAS BEEN USED FOR CENTURIES TO CONDITION HAIR. APPLIED REGULARLY, IT ADDS LUSTRE TO DARK HAIR.

It is claimed that rosemary plants grown in northern regions have a superior flavour for culinary use, compared to the southern-grown plants. However, both southern and northern European countries have many traditional recipes using rosemary. For some individual tastes, rosemary's pungency and strength of flavour is rather overpowering for certain foods. When using the herb as an ingredient in food, the leaves should always be chopped finely, unless you are using whole sprigs of rosemary, which can then be removed from the cooked dish. Whole sprigs of rosemary can be added to oil and vinegar to make herb-scented storecupboard condiments or herb marinades for meat or cheese.

The Italians use rosemary with roast meats, poultry, vegetables, barbecues and breads, such as *schiacciata*. This type of bread is baked in a large shallow dish and cut into wedges or chunks and eaten with grilled meats or salads. The bread may also be split and filled.

Marinated goat's cheese

In this recipe, rosemary is used with other herbs to add a subtle flavour to cheese, but you may like to use just one herb, or create your own mixture.

4–6 small, firm, fresh goat's cheeses
Olive oil
A bunch of fresh mixed herbs: rosemary, bay, thyme and marjoram
2 whole garlic cloves (optional)

Put the whole cheeses into a jar with a spring-top seal. Pour the olive oil over to completely cover the cheese. Tuck whole sprigs and leaves of the herbs into the jar. Then add the garlic cloves, if you are using them. Seal the top and store in a cool place for several days before eating, so the cheeses will absorb the flavour of the herbs. The cheeses stay fresh and preserved for a long time when covered by the oil.

FRESH GOAT'S CHEESE IS A DELICIOUS TREAT, MADE EVEN MORE SPECIAL WHEN PRESERVED WITH ROSEMARY AND OTHER HERBS.

Schiacciata
•

MAKES ABOUT 10 PIECES

1 level teaspoon easy-blend dried yeast
Pinch of salt
1 lb (450 g) strong, unbleached, white flour
½ pint (300 ml) warm water
Olive oil
2 sprigs of fresh rosemary, finely chopped
Coarse salt

In a large bowl, mix yeast and salt into the flour. Stir in water, then add 5 tablespoons of olive oil. Knead the dough until firm and smooth. Cover with a cloth and leave to rise for about 1 hour, until doubled in size.

Knock back the dough, and shape it into a large rectangle, about ½ inch (1 cm) thick. Put it on a large, well-oiled baking sheet. Cover, and leave to rise again. After about 20 minutes, brush the surface with more oil and prick it all over with a fork. Scatter rosemary leaves over the surface with plenty of coarse salt. Bake for about 30 minutes in a hot oven at 220°C (425°F) Mark 7, then turn the bread over, decrease the oven temperature to 180°C (350°F) Mark 4, and bake for a further 10 minutes. Cool on a wire rack, and brush with a little more oil to keep the crust soft while it cools.

THE ITALIANS USE ROSEMARY WITH GREAT GUSTO. THIS FLAT, PIZZA-LIKE BREAD IS MADE WITH OLIVE OIL AND SPRINKLED WITH ROSEMARY AND COARSE SALT.

Rosemary quail with red cabbage

SERVES 4

For this robust winter dish, it is best to make the cabbage the day before, and then reheat it.

1 tablespoon honey
1 tablespoon melted butter
2 sprigs of fresh rosemary, finely chopped
4 quail, cleaned, rinsed and patted dry
2 garlic cloves, each one peeled and
   chopped in half

Mix together the honey, melted butter and rosemary. Brush the mixture over each bird and put ½ garlic piece inside each bird. Roast uncovered in a hot oven at 220°C (425°F) Mark 7 for about 15 minutes. Check occasionally, and baste the birds with any juices. Serve the browned birds on a bed of red cabbage.

   You may also like to serve this dish with a gratin of potatoes, alongside the quails and red cabbage, and finish the meal with a lightly dressed, leafy green salad.

RED CABBAGE

1–2 tablespoons butter
1 medium red cabbage, thinly sliced
1 onion, thinly sliced
2 eating apples, cored, peeled and thinly sliced
1 garlic clove, crushed
3 tablespoons red wine vinegar
2 tablespoons soft brown sugar
Salt and pepper

Melt the butter in a heatproof casserole. Add the cabbage, onion and apple, and cook for a few minutes over a moderate heat, stirring constantly. Add the garlic, vinegar, sugar, and salt and pepper. Cover and transfer to the oven. Cook at 150°C (300°F) Mark 2 for 2–3 hours. Remove, cool, and refrigerate overnight.

Rosemary is often cooked with meat, as it helps counteract any over-richness or fattiness. The tough leaves of rosemary do not soften much with cooking, so it is often best to use a whole sprig of rosemary to add flavour, or else use several small sprigs tucked under the skin of a roast joint, such as a leg of lamb. The sprigs should be removed before serving the dish.

Lamb with rosemary crust

SERVES 6

Serve this beautiful and delicious dish with redcurrant jelly, new potatoes and a green vegetable.

A 3 lb (1.4 kg) leg of lamb with bone
A sprig of rosemary, roughly chopped
3 garlic cloves
Olive oil
Fresh rosemary sprigs, to garnish

ROSEMARY CRUST

6 tablespoons fresh breadcrumbs
1 tablespoon chopped, fresh parsley
1 tablespoon finely chopped, fresh rosemary
2 tablespoons melted butter
Salt and pepper

Make small slits in the skin of the lamb and tuck pieces of garlic in some of the slits and short rosemary pieces in others. Brush the meat with olive oil and roast in the oven at 180°C (350°F) Mark 4 for 45 minutes.

While the meat is cooking, make the crust by mixing all the rosemary crust ingredients together thoroughly. The easiest way to do this is to use a food processor.

Remove the lamb from the oven and spread the crust mixture over the skin. Return to the oven and cook for an additional 30 minutes. Serve on a bed of fresh rosemary as a garnish.

Sorrel

RUMEX ACETOSA

The fresh, bright green leaves of sorrel are some of the earliest to appear in the herb or vegetable garden. They look similar to spinach, but are more narrow and generally longer in leaf. Sorrel has a sharp, acid flavour and is used most often in soups and salads. The plant commonly grows wild in Europe and Asia, along roads, coastlines, and in damp meadows. It is also known by the common names of garden sorrel, common sorrel, meadow sorrel, sour grass and sour dock.

There are two other sorrel plants which are worth using as herbs. French sorrel, *Rumex scutatus*, is a superior herb and has round leaves. It grows into a large clump, providing leaves for a long season, especially if the flower heads are removed to encourage fresh growth. Buckler's sorrel is a small sorrel, with arrow-shaped leaves, and is excellent in mixed salads.

YOUNG SORREL LEAVES ADD A SHARP, LEMONY BITE TO SALADS. YOU NEED JUST A FEW OF THE LEAVES IN A MIXED GREEN SALAD.

Sorrel is a perennial plant, living for many years without needing much attention, though a top dressing of humus-rich soil or manure will improve the plant's vigour. The easiest way to propagate plants is by sowing seed in spring, and transplanting the small plants when they are big enough to handle. Sorrel prefers fairly moist soil and a sunny or lightly shaded position. The plants normally die back during the winter months, but they can be kept covered with a cloche to extend their growing season. The leaves are most tender when newly developed. Later in the season, they become coarse and stronger in flavour.

Sorrel's sharp, acid, lemony taste provides a contrast to bland or rich foods. Use raw sorrel in garden salads early in the season when their leaves are young and succulent. Since the herb is rather strong, it is best used with other leaves, such as lettuce, endive and chicory. Though it is used in greater quantities than many herbs, it is not suitable to be eaten like spinach or other leafy vegetables. It is best used as a green garnish for other dishes, such as a baked egg in cream on a bed of sorrel. Try using French sorrel, which is less acid, as a puréed vegetable.

Sorrel mixes well with spinach to make spring soups, and complements both eggs and fish. You may like to try using it in omelettes or in fish sauces. Greensauce, which is a mixture of sorrel leaves, vinegar and sugar, was used as an accompaniment to meat up until the eighteenth century in Britain. It was so well known that 'greensauce' became one of the common names for sorrel. Sorrel's bright green leaves become a dull, brownish pond-green when heated, but this can be prevented by shredding the leaves and adding them at the last minute to a dish.

SORREL MAKES A SUPERB ACCOMPANIMENT TO FISH. HERE, FRESH SALMON IS SERVED ON A BED OF SORREL AND SURROUNDED BY A FRAGRANT SAFFRON SAUCE.

Grilled salmon with saffron sauce on a bed of sorrel

•

SERVES 4

¾ lb (350 g) fresh sorrel leaves, washed and
    stripped from stems
1 tablespoon lemon juice
1 tablespoon water
3 tablespoons single cream
4 salmon steaks

Put the sorrel leaves, with the lemon juice and
water, into a saucepan over a moderate heat.
Cover and cook quickly until the leaves are
wilted and soft. Drain the sorrel and roughly
chop the leaves in the pan. Add the single
cream and keep warm.

    Grill the salmon steaks on both sides, until
the flesh flakes easily when tested with the tip of

a knife. Serve the fish on a bed of the sorrel and
pour the saffron sauce round it.

SAFFRON SAUCE

6 fl oz (180 ml) fish stock
A good pinch of saffron strands
1 dessert spoon lemon juice
1 oz (25 g) unsalted butter, diced
Salt and pepper

Pour the stock into a saucepan with the saffron
and lemon juice. Boil until slightly reduced,
then lower temperature and mix in the butter,
stirring until melted. Taste and season.

Rue

RUTA GRAVEOLENS

———— • ————

Rue is one of the most beautiful herbs, yet it has always had solemn connections. Perhaps because of its extreme bitter taste, rue has become known as the 'herb of repentance' and the 'herb of grace'. According to folklore, rue keeps one safe from witches and protects travellers on long journeys.

Rue is rarely used in foods, because it is poisonous in large quantities, however it has had many other uses in the past. It was once used as a 'strewing herb', but for the floors of prisons rather than homes, as it was thought to have strong powers over evil smells. Since the days of ancient Rome, rue has been associated with eyesight; it was thought to protect eyes from eye-strain and preserve good eyesight into old age. In fact, rutin, which is present in the leaves of the herb, is thought to be effective in treating abnormal blood pressure; however, a tisane made from the leaves is more or less undrinkable, unless heavily disguised by over-sweetening. Rue was one of the herbs thought to protect against the plague,

and it was included in flower bunches and nose-gays in the seventeenth and eighteenth centuries, particularly in bouquets for carrying into law courts and public places.

Rue is an aromatic, hardy evergreen, originating from southern Europe and northern Africa, but cultivated throughout Europe and the United States. It grows into a neat, shrubby bush, about 2 feet (60 cm) high. In spring, it should be severely clipped to encourage neat, new growth, otherwise its appearance can become straggly. Exercise caution when cutting the stems; many people are affected by the sap of the plant. If the sap remains on bare skin in strong sunshine, blisters can occur and the skin will appear burnt. This is not a serious condition, but the brown stains remain for quite awhile. Many other plants have this quality, so it is advisable to find out which ones may affect you.

The plant can be grown from seed or propagated by stem cuttings. During the summer, rue produces branches containing small, dull yellow flowers. The flowers are pretty when used in flower arrangements. Trimming the flowers from the plant will also keep rue tidy. The most popular variety is 'Jackman's Blue', which has a pronounced steely blue sheen to the foliage. Rue looks lovely growing with many herbs, particularly beside bronze-leaved plants, such as golden marjoram or golden feverfew. Rue does not have strict soil and position requirements, but it does prefer sun. It is also relatively disease-free.

The best way to use rue is in flower arrangements and garlands. Either dry the beautiful stems for dried arrangements or use the fresh leaves and flowers to add contrast and sparkle to fresh flower bouquets, especially those containing white- or cream-coloured flowers.

Rue garland

To make a fresh garland, you will need a large ring made from florist's foam, fresh branches of rue, and a collection of flowers. White chrysanthemums, yellow daisies, and lacy, white caraway flowers have been used here, but any similar flowers would look just as attractive.

Begin by soaking the foam ring in water until thoroughly damp. Then cut several stems of rue to the same length and push them into the foam ring, working all the way round, until the ring is evenly covered. Using one colour of flower at a time, push the flowers into place at regular intervals. Continue until the ring is full and no florist's foam is showing. Attach a wire or ribbon loop at the back to hang the garland in place.

RUE'S DELICATE AND COLOURFUL FOLIAGE IS HIGHLY EFFECTIVE WHEN USED WITH YELLOW AND WHITE SUMMER FLOWERS IN A FRESH GARLAND.

Sage

SALVIA OFFICINALIS

The large *Salvia* genus contains numerous sage plants, many which are highly decorative and are planted to bring colour to flower borders. The sage used as a herb, *Salvia officinalis*, does not often flower in northern climates, but has the best leaf for culinary and medicinal purposes. The soft, lanceolate, grey-green leaves and the pungent, slightly musty scent of the plant are familiar and easily recognizable. Sage retains its aroma well when dried, though, being an evergreen, it is not necessary to store the leaf this way. The best scent is in the leaf during the warm summer months.

Sage grows well in any well-drained soil, and prefers a sunny location. Though it can be grown from seed sown in spring, it is easier and quicker to buy small plants, or else take rooted pieces from an established plant. The greyish green-leaved type of sage never grows very tall, but it does spread slowly outward, creating a large plant after a few years.

Apart from the common culinary sage, there are two other types commonly seen in herb nurseries or garden centres. Purple sage has deep plum-red foliage with a greyish hue, and a tri-coloured type has splashes of red and cream variegation on the green leaves. There is also another, more uncommon, type of sage with golden-yellow variegated leaves. Purple sage is a decorative plant to grow among other herbs, and it looks particularly attractive planted next to silver-leaved plants. The purplish colour of the leaves seems to vary from plant to plant, and is dependent upon the plant's position in the sun. All the sages benefit from regular clipping to keep them healthy and in neat shape.

Sage dries well for winter flower arrangements and garlands. When trimming large plants, collect some branches to hang up to dry. The best time to do this is just before the flowers appear. As with other herbs, hang whole branches upside-down in a warm, airy place until fully dry. Sage takes a little longer to dry completely than some other herbs. You will be able to use the dried sage for culinary purposes, as well as for decorative displays. You can also make garlands and swags using fresh stems of the leaves, then allow them to dry naturally. If you do this, you will need to make the garlands very full because the leaves will shrink as they dry.

AFTER PICKING BUNCHES OF SAGE AND OTHER HERBS FROM YOUR GARDEN, GENTLY WASH THEM. AN OUTDOOR WASH BASIN, LIKE THE ONE SHOWN HERE, MAKES THE JOB EASIER.

PURPLE AND GREEN SAGE PLANTS PROVIDE STRIKING COLOUR OUTDOORS. PLANT THEM BESIDE BENCHES OR NEAR PATIOS WHERE THEY CAN BE APPRECIATED.

The name of the *Salvia* genus, derives from the Latin, meaning 'I am well', and the sage plant has always been considered to have all-round health-giving properties. For centuries, sage was thought to promote long life and was connected with success and fortune. The health of a sage plant in the garden supposedly reflected the fortunes of those who lived there. Sage tea has long been popular all over the world, even in tea-growing China. The leaves are thought to have digestive properties, which explains why they are used predominantly with rich, fatty meats, such as roast pork and duck. Dried and ground sage was once used as an early toothpaste to whiten teeth after smoking tobacco or drinking red wine; sage is still used in mouthwashes to strengthen gums and freshen the mouth.

The flavour of sage is strong and should be used with care in the kitchen. The leaves can be both dried and frozen successfully, but, if used fresh, they should be carefully washed beforehand. Sage is not generally used raw in salads, or as a garnish, because its flavour seems to suit hot, long-cooked dishes best. It is often used in cheeses and included in sausage mixtures. Try adding a handful of chopped sage and a few chopped black or green olives to a home-made bread dough for a delicious loaf to eat with soup or pasta. Or, fry sage leaves quickly in butter until they are crisp, but not burnt, and eat them with pork chops or sautéed potatoes.

The Italians have many classic dishes using sage, such as veal wrapped round sage leaves and deep-fried, batter-coated sage leaves. Calves' liver is sometimes flavoured with sage, and the herb is often used in hearty bean dishes. The English have few recipes which rely on the taste of sage, except for the popular sage and onion stuffing, which is traditionally eaten with roasted or grilled duck or pork.

Sage garland

To make a fresh sage garland, use either a damp ring made from florist's foam or use a wire shape covered with moss or straw. A moss or straw ring is the best one to use if you plan to allow the fresh garland to dry naturally, because, when the leaves shrink, the moss or straw makes a more attractive background than foam. Purple and green sages look lovely together, and both varieties retain their scent long after they have dried.

Simply cut stems of the sage and push them into the foam, or tuck them into the moss or straw, working evenly round the ring. If using a foam ring, stop when no foam shows through. If using a straw or moss ring, you may like to leave regular intervals bare. The garland makes a lovely decoration for a kitchen, and can be made at almost any time of the year.

A COOK'S GARLAND OF FRESH PURPLE AND GREEN SAGE BRANCHES CAN BE LEFT IN A WARM, AIRY PLACE, AND WILL LOOK JUST AS ATTRACTIVE WHEN DRY.

INSTEAD OF A SAGE AND ONION STUFFING, TRY THIS RED ONION SAUCE FLAVOURED WITH SAGE TO ACCOMPANY GRILLED DUCK BREASTS.

Duck breast with sage & onion sauce

SERVES 4

This recipe makes a sage and onion sauce, rather than the traditional stuffing, to serve with duck.

4 duck breasts, weighing about 6 oz (175 g) each

SAGE & ONION SAUCE

1 lb (450 g) red onions, finely chopped
2 oz (50 g) butter
2 oz (50 g) granulated sugar
1 tablespoon red wine vinegar
2 tablespoons chopped fresh sage leaves, preferably purple-leaved
Pinch of grated nutmeg
Pinch of ground cinnamon

To make the sauce, put the onions in a saucepan with the butter and cook gently over a low heat for about 15 minutes, until the onions are softened and the butter fully melted. Add the remaining sauce ingredients and stir well. Cover and simmer for a further 15 minutes. Remove the lid, and continue simmering until the sauce has reduced and thickened. Keep warm while you cook the duck.

Prick the surface of the duck breasts and either grill them quickly under a hot grill for about 5 minutes on each side, or roast, without oil, in the oven at 190°C (375°F) Mark 5, until just cooked but still pink inside. Cut each breast into slices lengthwise, and serve slightly fanned out on plates. Spoon about 2 tablespoons of the sauce on to each plate, beside the duck.

Salad Burnet

SANGUISORBA MINOR

Salad burnet, also called burnet, is one of the prettiest herbs, but it tends to get overlooked and is not as well known as it once was. The plant is a hardy perennial, native to most of Europe and spreading throughout the Northern Hemisphere. It is found growing wild on the chalk hills of Britain, and was taken to the United States by early settlers. It is sometimes known by the botanical name *Poterium sanguisorba*.

Salad burnet forms a low-growing plant with a central rosette of leaves. Delicate, reddish brown stems grow up through the leaves and unusual, greenish red, globular flowers appear at the top of each stem. The leaves are the part of the plant used as a culinary herb, and they have toothed edges, which also makes the plant very decorative in a herb garden.

The decorative properties of salad burnet were discovered in the seventeenth century, when herbs were used to fill the elaborate knot gardens so popular at the time. Salad burnet makes a perfect plant for growing in a formal herb garden, or among paving stones. It can also be grown at the front of a mixed border where it makes an attractive edging. The plant is happy in sun or partial shade, and in a range of soils, but seems to prefer limy soil. It is easily grown from seed, either sown *in situ* or in a small pot to transplant to its final position later. Young plants can also be bought from herb nurseries.

The taste of the salad burnet leaves is fresh, cool and slightly cucumber. For this reason, the herb has been used for centuries in green leafy salads and to add flavour to wine and ale. The herb is similar to borage, and can be used in the same way – by floating the leaves in summer drinks or wine cups. The chopped leaves can be used in soups, salad dressings, sauces, or added to mayonnaise to serve with chicken or cold, poached fish. Also, use whole leaves to decorate plates of cold food; the little, cut-edged, oval leaves make the most attractive garnishes.

THE CUCUMBER
FLAVOUR OF SALAD
BURNET BLENDS
WITH LEMON TO
MAKE A LIGHT AND
SIMPLE DRESSING
FOR A SLICED
CUCUMBER SALAD.

Salad burnet & lemon dressing

SERVES 6 OR MORE

Use this dressing on a green salad, a salad of cooked French beans, or with a simple dish
of peeled or sliced cucumbers.

Pared peel of 1 lemon, in long shreds
A small bunch of salad burnet leaves,
    finely chopped
6 tablespoons lemon juice
1 teaspoon clear honey
6 fl oz (180 ml) olive or groundnut oil
Salt and pepper

Take half the lemon peelings and chop them
very finely. Put the chopped peel and half the

salad burnet leaves in a small bowl or jar. Pour
over the lemon juice and add honey. Stir the
mixture well and leave for several hours for the
flavours to develop.

Strain the mixture and add the oil to it, bit by
bit, whisking well until thoroughly combined.
Add salt and pepper to taste.

Pour the dressing into a small glass jug or bowl
for serving, and decorate with the remaining
salad burnet and lemon peels.

Cotton Lavender

SANTOLINA CHAMAECYPARISSUS

Cotton lavender, or santolina, is in no way related to the lavender family, but one similarity is that it can be clipped to make a thick, low hedge. There are several species in the *Santolina* genus, almost all possessing crisp, silvery foliage. Some types have tight, neat, leaf growth, rather like coral, and others, such as the Italian *S. neapolitana*, have looser, more open, ferny foliage. *Santolina chamaecyparissus*, originally from southern France, forms a very dense mound of foliage. There is also a species called *S. virens* which has green rather than grey foliage. This type is widespreading and has pale lemon-yellow flowers, rather than the normal golden yellow. The button-like yellow flowers of cotton lavender appear in the middle of summer on single stems.

During the Tudor period in Britain, cotton lavender was commonly used to edge the elaborate knots and parterres beloved in the gardens of the time. Cotton lavender was chosen because it responded well to close clipping and could be cut into straight lines and geometric shapes. Cotton lavender prefers well-drained, slightly sandy soil, but is, generally, easy to please. Plants are easily propagated by taking small, heeled cuttings in the middle of summer for transplanting in autumn. Clipping later than mid-spring will result in the loss of that summer's flowers. However, it is often better to trim the plant in early spring, rather than to do it in autumn and leave the plant exposed to cold winter weather.

Either clipped close, or allowed to billow freely over a path edge, the plant is a beautiful addition to any herb garden or border. It has never been a culinary herb, but it has always been used as a protection for linen against moths and insects. The French call the herb *garde-robe*, and mix it with southernwood and lavender.

To dry cotton lavender for using in *garde-robe* mixtures, pot-pourris, or dried posies, cut the stems in the middle of summer and dry them as you would thyme (see page 130). You may want to cut fresh stems throughout the summer for using in fresh posies and flower arrangements. The pale colour of the leaves blends particularly well with pinks and mauves.

THE FERNY, GREY LEAVES OF COTTON LAVENDER PROVIDE A PERFECT BACKGROUND FOR PINK ROSEBUDS, PINK CARNATIONS AND SCENTED VIOLETS IN THIS POSY.

BUSHES OF COTTON LAVENDER CAN BE CLIPPED AND CUT QUITE SEVERELY TO MAKE A MINIATURE TOPIARY IN A POT.

Victorian cotton lavender posy

For this posy, you will need cotton lavender and small flowers: pink rosebuds, pink spray carnations and deep purple violets. In your hands, start with one rose in the centre, then surround it with cotton lavender. Working outwards and in a circle, add a row of violets, then a row of roses. Then add more cotton lavender and finish with a row of carnations. Tie the stems tightly with string, cover the string with a ribbon and complete with a bow, if desired. Trim the bottoms of all the stems.

Savory

SATUREJA

There are two distinct types of savory, summer savory, *Satureja hortensis,* and winter savory, *Satureja montana.* At first glance, both savorys look rather like hyssop or the more upright varieties of thyme. The flavour of the leaves and shoots is strong, slightly bitter and spicy, but summer savory is milder in flavour than its winter relative, and more often used as a culinary herb.

Winter savory is, however, more commonly seen in cultivation. It is a small, low-growing, almost evergreen herb with tough, wiry stems and small, narrow, grey-green leaves which densely cover the stem. Summer savory is also a small plant, but with bushy, hairy stems and dark green leaves. In summer, winter savory usually has rose-purple flowers and summer savory has lilac flowers. The flowers appear along the length of the stem, tucked in beside the leaves. Bees and insects are attracted to the flowers.

Both the savorys have been in cultivation for centuries. The ancient Romans were fond of a pungent sauce made from pounded savory leaves. The volatile oil, found in the leaves, was once used as a cure for digestive ailments and to relieve the pain of insect bites and stings.

Summer savory should be sown from seed in late spring, either where the plant is to grow, or else in small pots to be transplanted out later. Winter savory can also been sown from seed, but it is often available as a small plant from herb nurseries. Winter savory adapts well to growing in a tub or container where it makes a pretty, small bush, curving over the edge of the pot. Both types like well-drained soil and sun.

Savory is often included in French, Swiss and German cuisine. It can be included in soups, stuffings, or in meat, egg, cheese or fish dishes. There has long been an affinity between savory and beans. The French often plant savory beside rows of beans in the vegetable garden, and the two plants are then combined in the kitchen. Beans are often cooked with a sprig of savory as a flavouring, rather like peas or new potatoes cooked with mint. Savory has been used in France to cover small white cheeses, though rosemary is now more commonly used. Also, like many herbs, savory makes a useful and delicious ingredient in vinegar.

Savory vinegar

Collect fresh leaves of summer or winter savory and put them into a sterilized, sealable jar. Pour over gently warmed white wine or cider vinegar. Seal the jar securely, and leave for several weeks before using.

Use the vinegar in salad dressings, or add a small spoonful to soups or stews to add piquancy. The vinegar makes a particularly nice touch to thick dried bean soups.

WINTER SAVORY GROWS HAPPILY IN A CONTAINER PLACED ON A BALCONY, TERRACE OR WINDOW-SILL. THE PALE FLOWERS APPEAR FROM SUMMER TO AUTUMN.

Broad beans in savory sauce

·

SERVES 4

1 lb (450 g) shelled broad beans
A whole sprig of fresh summer savory
½ oz (15 g) butter
1 tablespoon plain flour
¼ pint (150 ml) milk
4 sprigs of summer savory, finely chopped
¼ pint (150 ml) single cream
Pinch of grated nutmeg
Salt and pepper

Boil the beans briefly in water with the whole sprig of savory. Drain, but reserve a little of the cooking water. Set the beans aside. Then, melt the butter in a large saucepan, add the flour and cook for a few minutes over a moderate heat, stirring well. Add the milk, bit by bit, stirring constantly until the sauce thickens. Add a little of the bean water and cook for 5 minutes or so. Then add the chopped savory to the sauce, and stir in the cream. Taste and season with nutmeg and salt and pepper.

Pour the beans into the cream sauce, and reheat for a few seconds. Serve the dish immediately while still warm.

BROAD BEANS AND SAVORY HAVE LONG BEEN CULINARY PARTNERS, AND SAVORY IS KNOWN AS THE BEAN HERB. HERE, THE TWO INGREDIENTS COMBINE IN A CREAMY DISH.

Tansy

TANACETUM VULGARE

A common roadside wild flower of northern Europe, tansy is a very attractive herb with its clustered flower heads of tight, yellow, button-like flowers. Tansy was taken from Britain to the United States by early settlers and is widely naturalized there. Tansy has been given many different common names over the years by country dwellers, who often see the cheerful yellow flowers along dusty lanes and river banks. Traveller's rest, bachelor's buttons, bitter buttons, golden buttons and ginger plant are just a few colloquial names, but every country seems to have its own.

At various times in the plant's history, tansy has been used as a culinary herb, a dye plant, a medicine and a fragrant herb for household use. The flavour of tansy is exceedingly bitter, and not commonly used in the kitchen today, though it was very popular up until the seventeenth century. Tansy was traditionally used in an Easter dish, which, from old recipes, seems to have been a kind of cake or pancake, but which must have been more of penance than a pleasure to eat. The plant's name derives from a Greek word meaning 'immortality' so this is probably the reason it was eaten at Easter. There are also many old recipes for dishes known as 'tansies', usually eaten as puddings, but generally not containing the herb itself. Before the advent of refrigeration, meat was often rubbed with tansy leaves to repel flies. It was also used as a 'strewing herb' for floors, because, with its powerful scent and plant oils, it was considered a disinfectant. An infusion of tansy is mildly narcotic, and not recommended, though it was once prescribed as a tea for sick children and to help sufferers of rheumatism.

Tansy makes an interesting perennial herb to grow in a garden. The leaves are dark green with serrated edges and have a pungent scent. But beware, once planted in a garden, tansy spreads rapidly and can be almost impossible to eradicate if it establishes itself in an undesirable place. Tansy spreads outward by means of stolons. It

TANSY FLOWERS
ARE ONE OF THE
EASIEST AND
BEST FLOWERS
TO DRY FOR
ARRANGEMENTS.
THE STEMS STAY
STIFF, AND THE
YELLOW COLOUR
REMAINS TRUE.

can be grown from seed, or bought as a small plant, but it should never be taken from the wild. Tansy prefers rich, moist soil.

Tansy flowers are quite hard and dry, even when fresh, so they are perfect to use in flower arrangements. Pick the flowers when they are still a strong yellow in colour, and before they acquire a dull brown tinge. Hang the stems in an airy and dry place until the flowers feel completely hard and desiccated. The stems will stay beautifully stiff after drying, which allows them to be manipulated in arrangements. Try mixing the subtle, deep yellow flowers with strong blue and purple flowers. For a softer, more rural, effect, use dried tansy with wheat, grasses, and flowers and herbs with cream or beige colours.

Dried tansy arrangement

This is an informal arrangement displayed in an old terracotta plant pot. Stems of dried tansy have been combined with bunches of deep purple-blue larkspur, lavender, for scent, and little bundles of green wheat. The tansy has been placed in the foreground, with a few stems of the taller yellow yarrow (*Achillea*) in the background. A small, cluster-headed variety of everlasting (*Eryngium*) has been used to fill empty spaces. Arranged compactly, the flowers and grasses will stand in the pot without any florist's mechanics, but, if you like, support the stems using dry florist's foam pushed securely into the base of the flowerpot.

Thyme

THYMUS

There are over 30 different varieties of thyme and they fall into two main categories, relating to the way in which they grow. The upright forms develop into small, shrubby bushes, while the low-growing, creeping varieties spread out across the ground and are ideal for planting between paving cracks. The main culinary varieties belong to the upright group; the low-growing thymes being used mostly as decorative additions to the garden.

Common thyme, *Thymus vulgaris,* is also known as garden thyme. It is the one most often used in the kitchen, but can be grown as an ornamental feature in the garden. It has aromatic, dark green leaves with clusters of mauve flowers. The golden-leaved variety is *Thymus vulgaris* 'Aureus'. The lemon-scented thyme, *Thymus* x *citrioderus,* has a similar appearance to the common thyme but with broader, lemon-scented leaves and slightly larger flowers in a pale lilac colour. This type is

LOW, SPREADING THYMES FORM SCENTED CARPETS, WHICH CAN BE WALKED UPON. THEY ARE ALSO USEFUL FOR COVERING LOW WALLS OR BANKS.

FRESH THYME AND GOLDEN MARJORAM ARE INTERWOVEN IN A VINE GARLAND TO MAKE A SCENTED DECORATION FOR THE KITCHEN.

more often used as an ingredient in sweet foods and pot-pourris.

Wild thyme, *Thymus serpyllum*, is now botanically known as *Thymus drucei*. It has many common names, including mother of thyme, creeping thyme and mountain thyme. The flowers are soft mauve-pink in colour, but plants have been developed with flowers ranging in colour from white to deep purple and crimson. The leaves are narrow and grey-green, but there are also silver and gold variegated leaf varieties, as well as soft, woolly-leaved types.

Another popular thyme, *Thymus herba-barona*, is known as caraway thyme because its scent is similar to the caraway herb. It is low-spreading and beautifully scented, but is best used in the garden rather than the kitchen.

All the thymes have a very attractive growth habit. The Greek name for thyme, *thymon*, is thought to derive from either a Greek verb, meaning 'to burn', or from a noun, meaning 'courage'; the upright thymes, with their spiky growth, topped by vivid flowers, do look somewhat like flames. Thymes attract insects, bees and butterflies, and creeping thymes make fragrant carpets underfoot. The plant is certainly an invaluable asset to a garden.

All thymes like a sunny position in well-drained, fertile soil. It is a good idea to replace them after three or four years when the growth tends to become straggly. Flowers will appear throughout summer.

Thyme should be picked on a fine day, just before it comes into flower. The best time of day to harvest it is after the dew has dried, but before the hot sun has evaporated the plant's essential oils. Use fresh thyme as a herb in food, or as an aromatic decoration for the home.

Thyme garland

·

During the summer months, make garlands of fresh herbs for hanging in the kitchen. Use a ready-made, twisted vine or straw base and simply tuck small bunches of thyme in among the twigs or straw. Work evenly in a circular movement round the garland. Hang immediately, or leave to dry in a dark place.

The method for drying and storing thyme is the same for many other herbs which can be preserved in this way, such as rosemary, marjoram or sage. The old-fashioned way to dry herbs was simply to hang bunches of each different type of herb in a warm kitchen or near a heat source until they were dry.

They were often left there and used when needed, being conveniently near the cooking pot. This may be a picturesque way of drying herbs, but it is not really the best way. Herbs left hanging for any length of time in an exposed place get dusty, musty, and rapidly lose their flavour. You can dry herbs in bunches this way, if you have a kitchen stove or range which is a constant heat source. Otherwise, hang the herbs in a warm cupboard or warm, airy place until the leaves are brittle and fully dried.

The most efficient method is to lay stems of herbs on racks or trays in a single layer. Then put the trays in an oven on a very low setting or in a warm, airy place. If the leaves turn brown, rather than stay green, then the heat source was too intense. In humid northern climates, check that the herbs do not go mouldy or mildewed, especially if there are a few days of rain while completing the drying process. It may be worth experimenting with a microwave oven for the purpose of drying herbs – some manufacturers give instructions for doing this, but it may depend on the type of microwave oven you have.

Once you have stems of fully dried thyme, then the leaves should be stripped off the stems. Do this by rubbing the leaves through your fingers over a large shallow bowl or tray, or inside a paper bag. Once all the leaves are stripped, they should be packed into small, airtight jars, boxes or tins. If the jars are made from transparent glass, then, once filled, they should be stored somewhere dark. Light causes the herb to fade and lose flavour. Label or mark each variety, so you do not mistake one for another. Thyme only keeps well for a few months, and it is sensible to check all stored herbs regularly. It is a good idea to discard any herbs that have lost flavour or smell musty and old.

An excellent non-culinary use for thyme is to tie up the dried stalks to make an aromatic bundle for burning in a fireplace. Tie them in bundles in the summer, after you have stripped them of the leaves, and keep them in a dry, dark place until ready for use in late autumn and winter. Another idea is to make pot-pourris or bath sachets filled with thyme. The oil from the herb is antiseptic and invigorating; thyme baths are said to be helpful for aches, bruises and swellings. Other ingredients can also be added if desired.

A SMALL BUNCH OF THYME HANGS UP TO DRY BETWEEN A BUNCH OF MIXED HERBS AND A BUNCH OF SAGE. A DRY, DARK AND AIRY SHED IS AN IDEAL PLACE TO DRY HERBS.

LIKE ALL DRIED HERBS, THYME SHOULD BE STORED IN BOXES OR TINS IN A COOL, DARK PLACE. USE DRIED THYME IN STEWS, CASSEROLES AND POT-POURRIS.

Thyme bath bags
•

4 tablespoons oatmeal
2 tablespoons dried thyme
1 tablespoon red rose petals
10 crumbled bay leaves

Mix all the ingredients together and spoon into little cheesecloth or muslin bags. Tie them securely and use one in each bath, either hanging from the tap or swirled in the water. The bags can usually be used twice.

JELLIES, OILS AND VINEGARS, FLAVOURED WITH THYME, ARE GOOD STORECUPBOARD INGREDIENTS, AND MAKE LOVELY GIFTS.

Lemon thyme-flavoured jelly

Use a basic recipe for a sharp apple jelly, and add in extra lemon juice. At the boiling stage, add whole fresh stems of lemon thyme, removing them when the setting point is reached. After skimming off the foam, and just before potting up the jelly into little containers, add more fresh chopped thyme leaves or a whole stem of fresh thyme, if preferred, and pot and cover according to the recipe. Do not used dried lemon thyme in this recipe as it will produce a rather musty-tasting jelly.

Thyme oils & vinegars

Herb-flavoured oils and vinegars are lovely storecupboard ingredients to have for cooking. For a thyme-flavoured oil, simply add a sprig of thyme to good quality olive or groundnut oil and leave for several months before using.

For a vinegar, use good white wine vinegar and heat a small amount to the boiling point. Pour this over fresh, chopped thyme leaves. Leave to cool, then add to the remaining vinegar. In each bottle place a sprig of fresh thyme and cork or seal firmly.

Thyme retains its flavour after long cooking, and for this reason it is one of the most useful herbs to use in slow-cooked casseroles or for roasts. It is also delicious with game and beef, and an essential ingredient for a bouquet garni to add to broths, stocks and stews.

Dried thyme is a good substitute for fresh thyme in cooked food, so it is one herb which is well suited for use in many winter recipes. Add a whole sprig of fresh or dried thyme to dishes, then remove it from the dish before serving. The leaves can be chopped very finely if you prefer, but avoid using the tough stems.

Lemon thyme, with its fresh, clean lemony scent and flavour, is one of the most useful varieties for the kitchen. It is usually best to grow this herb, as it is difficult to find in food shops. The flavour is quite pronounced and combines well with chicken and white fish. Lemon thyme also makes a delicious jelly to eat with lamb and other roast meats.

Thyme's warm taste is frequently used in Mediterranean dishes. Wild thyme grows throughout the olive groves of Greece, Italy and France and the two ingredients make natural partners. A good way to improve the taste of imported olives is to cover them with thyme-scented oil and leave them to soak up the flavour.

Greek olives with thyme

Choose the largest green olives you can find, preferably with stones. Put them into a wide-necked jar with a sealable lid, and add about 5 peeled garlic cloves and about 4 lemon segments. Take a small bunch of fresh thyme and split it into little sprigs. Tuck these down among the olives and then pour olive oil in, to cover. Close the top and leave for several weeks. When you serve the olives, as an hors-d'oeuvre or in a salad, add a little extra finely chopped, fresh thyme over them.

PLAIN OLIVES CAN BE TRANSFORMED BY THE FLAVOUR OF FRESH THYME, GARLIC AND LEMON. SERVE THEM WITH CHEESE OR DRINKS BEFORE A MEAL.

Nasturtium

TROPAEOLUM MAJUS

The nasturtium is an annual plant native to South America but now grown all over the world. Both dwarf forms and a trailing variety are available and the plant thrives in poor soil and a sunny position. Nasturtiums should be sown from seed in the spring and they flower throughout the summer, seeding themselves readily. They are hardy and can be sown straight into the ground. Their trailing and climbing nature makes them suitable for covering trellises, fences and banks, but they also look effective growing in pots in greenhouses or in hanging baskets. The more compact dwarf strains make lovely additions to flower beds, path edges or rock gardens.

Nasturtium flowers are usually orange or golden-yellow with shades ranging from pale lemon to deep rust-red. They are faintly scented, have a long spur, and are long lasting when cut. The smooth, medium green leaves are veined outward from the centre and have curved edges.

Traditionally, nasturtiums were used as a remedy against scurvy because the leaves (which taste hot and peppery) have a very high vitamin C content. The fresh flowers and leaves can be added to salads. To prepare the flower heads for eating, ensure they are umblemished and have not been sprayed. Do not wash them if at all possible, as the delicate petals are easily bruised.

The bright, cheerful flowers also make pretty arrangements: use them simply without other flowers, as the hot colours are quite powerful. A bunch of large yellow and orange nasturtium flowers in a brightly coloured vase adds a brilliant sunny glow to any room.

A HANDFUL OF NASTURTIUM LOOKS BEST ARRANGED SIMPLY IN A JUG OR PLAIN-COLOURED VASE. HERE, THE VIBRANT COLOURS OF THE FLOWERS PROVIDE A STRIKING CONTRAST TO A GREEN JUG.

Summer salad

Make the basis of the salad from a mixture of variously coloured and shaped salad leaves, such as lettuce, young spinach and sorrel. Toss in a handful of nasturtium flowers and add fresh herbs according to taste. If you like the peppery taste of nasturtium leaves, add these as well. A few heads of blue borage flowers provide a lovely colour contrast to the nasturtiums. Make a simple vinaigrette dressing. Just before serving, toss with the salad in a large serving bowl.

THE BRILLIANT ORANGE FLOWERS OF NASTURTIUMS COMBINE WITH BLUE BORAGE FLOWERS AND MIXED LEAVES TO MAKE AN EXCITING AND DELICIOUS SALAD.

THE GREEN AND WHITE FOLIAGE OF VARIEGATED NASTURTIUM ADDS EXTRA COLOUR TO A POT OF GROWING HERBS.

In addition to a beautiful appearance and a peppery taste, the nasturtium flowers, which bloom from the middle of summer to early autumn, have a sweet smell. The leaves and stems also have a strong scent when they are crushed. One old common name for nasturtium is Indian cress, which suggests that the plant was always used for culinary as well as decorative purposes.

Scented flowers and leaves always add a lovely natural touch to food. Nasturtium flowers can be used as edible garnishes for all kinds of dishes, but the plant can also be more versatile. Chopped flowers mix well with cream cheese for sandwiches or canapés, and the whole flower heads can be stuffed with soft cheese and nuts. In parts of Britain, until recently, the unripe seeds and flower buds of the nasturtium plant were pickled and used as a substitute for capers. The flavour was appreciated by the British because of their taste for hot and fiery chutneys. To try pickled nasturtium seeds, just follow the recipe here. It is an easy pickle to make.

Pickled nasturtium seeds

Collect a number of nasturtium seeds. They need to be young, tender, and still fresh and green. Once they have ripened beyond this point, they cannot be used. The best time to pick them is just after the flowers finish.

Pack the seeds into a clean, sterilized, small, wide-mouthed jar that can be sealed. Measure enough vinegar to suit the capacity of your jar. Flavour the vinegar with salt and black peppercorns and boil in a saucepan. The choice of vinegar is up to you – distilled or malt vinegars are very strong in taste, but cider or wine vinegar is mild. Pour the boiling vinegar over the seeds to cover, and seal the jar immediately. Leave the jar in a cool place for 6 weeks before using.

Pickled nasturtium seeds can be used as a garnish, or else as a substitute for capers on pizzas, in sauces, or in snacks and hors-d'oeuvres. Once you have opened the jar, it is best to use all the seeds within a few days time.

Stuffed nasturtium flowers

·

SERVES 4

This recipe makes a pretty and delicious summer pudding. Gather the flowers when they are just fully open and fresh. Avoid washing them if possible, but do ensure they are unblemished, free from pesticides, and have no hidden insects lurking behind the flower spur.

2 oz (50 g) granulated sugar
6 oz (175 g) ricotta cheese
1 drop pure almond essence
4 oz (100 g) blanched almonds, finely chopped
4 fl oz (100 ml) double cream, stiffly whipped
16 nasturtium flowers

Lightly beat the sugar into the ricotta cheese and add the almond essence. Toast the chopped almonds in a hot oven or under a grill, watching carefully to make sure they do not burn. Remove, and leave them to cool.

Fold the whipped cream into the cheese mixture and add the toasted almonds. Taste and adjust sweetening and flavouring, if desired. Take small spoonfuls of the mixture and stuff each flower. Arrange the flowers on a serving plate. Serve as a pudding or afternoon snack with crisp biscuits, a fresh fruit sauce or a colourful mixed fruit salad.

OFFER SPECIAL GUESTS THIS IMPRESSIVE PUDDING MADE FROM NASTURTIUM FLOWERS, WHICH ARE FILLED WITH FLUFFY CREAM CHEESE AND CRUNCHY TOASTED ALMONDS.

Sweet Violet

VIOLA ODORATA

The sweet violet, also called the garden violet, is a member of the large *Viola* genus, but it is *Viola odorata* which has become an important herb for its scent. Violets have always been surrounded by symbolism, and they were used in the elaborate 'language of flowers' in the late nineteenth century. The tiny blooms have been used in medicines, liqueurs, sweetmeats and salads because of their subtle and haunting scent.

Sweet violets are hardy perennials, growing wild throughout Europe, Asia and North Africa. They prefer cool and shady conditions, such as light woodlands, meadows, banks or hedges in the spring and summer, but more open conditions in the winter. They do need to be shielded from the heat of fierce summer sun, and they require a rich, moist, well-drained soil.

Plants grow to about 4–6 inches (10–15 cm), and have heart-shaped leaves and small, purple, spring flowers. There are varieties with white- or rose-coloured flowers. It is often beneficial to remove flowers as they fade; this will ensure a succession of blooms. The root of the flower sends out long runners along the ground. The runners take root and form rosettes of leaves, which can then be propagated.

In medieval times, all kinds of dishes were extravagantly decorated with violet flowers and petals, both fresh and crystallized. Sweet violet water was a popular gift, and violet oil was a

Crystallized violets

For this method, you will need powdered gum arabic and rosewater, both available from a chemist. Pick as many violet blooms as you wish to crystallize. Then dissolve 1 tablespoon of gum arabic in 1 tablespoon of rosewater and leave until the solution becomes a paste. Using a small brush, paint each violet all over with the solution, then dip the flowers in caster sugar, ensuring that every bit of petal is covered. Leave to dry and crisp on a wire rack in a warm place. Store the petals in an airtight container, and use them on puddings as an edible garnish.

CRYSTALLIZED VIOLET FLOWERS ARE FUN TO MAKE AND HIGHLY EFFECTIVE AS DECORATIONS ON SWEET DISHES.

USE CRYSTALLIZED VIOLETS LAVISHLY ON THIS OLD-FASHIONED BROWN BREAD ICE-CREAM, AND SERVE WITH CRISP WAFERS OR BISCUITS.

cosmetic and a healing lotion. A syrup made from violets was considered a medicine for purging the stomach and, sometimes, for reviving lost appetites. Violet petals do, in fact, contain an alkaloid which can work as an emetic, but, presumably, very large quantities would be necessary for this purpose.

Sweet violets have been cultivated as a commercial crop for centuries. They have been used for perfume and toiletries, and flavourings for drinks, such as the sweet, purple-coloured liqueur, *parfait amour*. In Victorian times, flower-sellers sold small bunches of violets on the streets of large cities. Women would pin the flowers to their hats or dresses and men would wear them as buttonholes.

Today, sweet violets are often used as ingredients in sweet foods, as beautiful decorations for food, or in miniature posies and fresh flower arrangements. Crystallized violets are still one of the most favourite culinary ways to use the exquisite blooms.

Brown bread ice-cream with violets

SERVES 6

½ pint (300 ml) double cream, whipped
6 oz (125 g) caster sugar
Few drops vanilla essence
6 oz (125 g) wholemeal breadcrumbs, toasted
2 oz (50 g) granulated sugar
4 tablespoons water
2 tablespoons crushed crystallized violets

Beat the cream and caster sugar together until light and thick. Flavour with the vanilla, and freeze until it becomes mushy. Dissolve the granulated sugar in the water and bring to the boil. Let the syrup boil for a few minutes, then take off the heat and let cool. Mix the breadcrumbs with the cooled syrup. Then quickly mix the syrup into the half-frozen ice-cream. Freeze until completely solid. Thickly scatter each portion with the violet pieces.

Herb Glossary

Achillea millefolium. Yarrow. A common perennial with tough stems and clusters of white flowers. It was once used in tisanes and for healing wounds. The herb makes a pretty garden plant, and the flowers, which dry well, are useful in flower arrangements. The leaves can be used in salads.

Alchemilla vulgaris. Lady's mantle. A hardy herbaceous perennial plant with soft, pretty leaves and clusters of tiny, lime-green flowers. The plant can be used in dried or fresh flower arrangements, and was once used to treat female illnesses, hence its common name.

Artemisia vulgaris. Mugwort. A silver-leaved perennial with insignificant green flowers. Like its relatives wormwood and southernwood, it can be used in sachets and posies to repel moths. It was once used to make a tea and was placed in shoes to prevent tired feet on long journeys.

Calaminthus officinalis. Calamint. A small, neat perennial with tiny, reddish purple flowers and soft, hairy leaves. It has an aromatic, slightly peppermint, scent. It is an ideal herb to grow among paving stones on a terrace or in a herb garden, and it attracts bees.

Carthamus tinctorius. Safflower. A thistle-like annual with rich orange flowers. The somewhat bitter-tasting seeds are used to make the popular cooking oil, and the flowers are used as a dye and food colouring. The dried flower heads are excellent for winter arrangements.

Chenopodium bonus-henricus. Good King Henry. A leafy perennial herb, once commonly grown as a vegetable. The leaves are rich in vitamins and iron, and can be used raw in salads or cooked like spinach. The young and tender flower buds are also edible. It still grows wild in Britain.

Cymbopogon citratus. Lemon grass. Grown in India and the tropics, this is one grass, among several, cultivated for its oil. It has a strong citrus scent and is peeled and chopped for flavouring food. When dried, lemon grass makes a lovely addition to pot-pourris and sweet bags.

Eupatorium purpureum. Gravelroot or Joe-pye weed. A tall perennial plant, native to North America and thriving in moist soil. It has medium green, vanilla-scented foliage and large, rosy pink flowers. It is an astringent and diuretic, and its past uses have been primarily medicinal.

Galega officinalis. Goat's rue. A large, perennial, leguminous plant with pale mauve or white flowers and attractive foliage. It was used in the Middle Ages as a cure for the plague and was once considered a good animal fodder. Today, it is used as an attractive and old-fashioned garden plant.

Helichrysum angustifolium. Curry plant. A silver-leaved perennial shrub with yellow, button-like flowers. The leaves smell strongly of curry when crushed, but are not used in curry powder. The dried leaves can be used in pot-pourris, and the dried stems in flower arrangements.

Inula helenium. Elecampane. A tall perennial plant with handsome leaves and small, sunflower-like, yellow flowers. It makes a powerful antiseptic and was once used in veterinary medicines and for chest ailments. The root was also candied and made into a tonic.

Malva sylvestris. Common mallow. A decorative perennial, with heart-shaped leaves and attractive clear pink flowers. It is a member of a large family which includes the musk mallow, marsh mallow and hibiscus. The leaves make a good tisane, which helps throat complaints.

Marrubium vulgare. Horehound. A bushy perennial with white flowers and silver-frosted foliage. It provides a good contrast of foliage texture in the garden. Once used to make a cough sweet and a tisane for chest complaints, as well as a cure for the bite of a mad dog.

Myrtus communis. Myrtle. A small-leaved evergreen shrub or tree with aromatic foliage and vanilla-scented white flowers. The oil, myrtol, from the plant is used in perfumery and medicines. Fresh leaves are used in stuffings for poultry. Dried leaves and flowers may be added to pot-pourris.

Pimpinella anisum. Aniseed. An aromatic annual with feathery leaves and typically umbellifer white flowers. The anise-flavoured leaves can be eaten in salads or with fish, and the sweet, ripe seeds are used for flavouring cakes, breads, sweets and liqueurs.

Polygonum bistorta. Bistort. A low, creeping perennial with blue-green leaves and deep pink flower spikes. The seeds are loved by birds. In northern England, bistort was once used in an Easter pudding. Bistort makes a pretty, old-fashioned plant for a herb garden.

Potentilla reptans. Cinquefoil. A low-growing perennial with delicate, five-fingered leaves and yellow flowers. In the past, the roots and leaves have been used in mouthwash, fishbait and in sinister witchcraft recipes. The herb makes an extremely pretty garden plant.

Primula veris. Cowslip. Once a common perennial, cowslip produces downy leaves and clusters of scented, yellow, spring flowers. At one time it was used in puddings, wines and cosmetics. It was also included in flower balls for spring festivals. Now quite rare, it is prized for the flower bed.

Sambucus nigra. Elderflower. A small tree with tiny white flowers. All parts of the tree are used, including roots, bark, flowers, leaves and berries. Other species of elder have poisonous parts. The muscat grape flavour of the white flowers is used to enhance wine, puddings and preserves.

Saponaria officinalis. Soapwort. A sometimes invasive perennial, with bright pink flowers and a creeping rhizomatous root. The leaves and roots are soaked in water to make a natural and highly effective cleansing agent for delicate fabrics, and to make skin cleansers and shampoos.

Stachys officinalis. Betony. A perennial plant which grows in woodlands and meadows, and has spikes of reddish purple flowers. At one time, the leaves were used to make a herbal tobacco. The leaves can be used to make a tea, and the herb is reputed to calm nerves and cure headaches.

Symphytum officinale. Comfrey. This perennial has white or pink to blue flowers and bristly leaves. In the past, the leaves have been used to help set bones, and the roots were made into infusions for pulmonary complaints. The dried leaves are used in tea, and the dried root is used in wine.

Tanacetum balsam. Alecost or Costmary. A perennial and relative of tansy, which has a straggly habit and untidy yellow flowers. It was once used for a tonic, as a 'strewing herb' and to flavour beer. The leaves are sweet and spicy, and can be used in pot-pourris and as insect repellents.

Taraxacum officinale. Dandelion. A well-known perennial with soft, toothed leaves and golden flowers. The young leaves make a delicious bitter salad ingredient and the flowers are used to make wine. The juice from the stem is a diuretic, and the dried ground root is a good coffee substitute.

Trigonella foenum-graecum. Fenugreek. An ancient cultivated perennial with fragrant, cream-coloured flowers. The oval, bitter leaves are sometimes cooked as a vegetable. The seeds are used as a spice and curry powder blend. The herb is also used to flavour imitation maple syrup.

Urtica dioica. Nettle. A perennial and a tenacious weed. The leaves sting when touched, but the cooked young leaves are delicious, as a vegetable or in soups. The leaves contain iron and make a good tonic tea. The fibrous stems and leaves were once used for making cloth and paper.

Valerianella locusta. Lamb's lettuce or Corn salad. A small, biennial plant with a cluster of soft leaves and pale mauve flowers. It can be overwintered and is surprisingly hardy. It is grown as a useful salad crop for winter or early spring, and is particularly delicious with beetroot.

Verbena officinalis. Vervain. A perennial or annual, with small, dark green leaves on strong, stiff stems, bearing pale mauve flowers. It has been associated with magic and witchcraft. It is an astringent and used in hair tonics or eye-washes, and in tea. It is meant to cure headaches.

SOAPWORT MAKES A LOVELY OLD-FASHIONED HERB FOR THE GARDEN WITH ITS TALL REDDISH STEMS AND CLUSTERS OF SUMMER FLOWERS.

Index

Figures in **bold** indicate illustrations

Acknowledgements

The publishers would like to thank the following for their help in
the preparation of this volume:

Vicki Robinson for the Index

For gold and green pots on pages 77 and 124
Mondian Ltd
Swindon

For photographic locations
Essenbourne Manor Hotel, Andover

Hollington Herb Nursery
Wootton Hill, Newbury
Berkshire

Picture Credits

With the exception of the photographs listed below,
all photographs in this book
are by Di Lewis © Salamander Books Ltd.
Photographs are credited on the page: (T) Top, (B) Bottom.

Harry Smith Horticultural Collection: 16 (T), 34 (T), 100 (T),
126, 138 (T)

David Squire: 18 (T), 22 (T), 80 (T), 88 (B), 96, 112 (T)